HERO CATS

*True Stories of
Daring Feline Deeds*

HERO CATS

True Stories of

Daring Feline Deeds

by Eric Swanson

A High Tide Press Book

**Andrews McMeel
Publishing**

Kansas City

HERO CATS
TRUE STORIES OF DARING FELINE DEEDS
copyright ©1998 by Eric Swanson.
All rights reserved. Printed in Singapore.
No part of this book may be used or reproduced in any manner
whatsoever without written permission except in the case of reprints in
the context of reviews. For information write to:
Andrews McMeel Publishing, an Andrews McMeel Universal company,
4520 Main Street, Kansas City, Missouri 64111.

www.andrewsmcmeel.com

98 99 00 01 02 TWP 10 9 8 7 6 5 4 3 2 1

Cover Photograph © G. K. & Vikki Hart/Image Bank
Design by Robbin Gourley
Edited by Lisa MacDonald

Library of Congress Cataloging-in-Publication Data
Swanson, Eric, 1959–
Hero Cats : true stories of daring feline deeds / by Eric Swanson.
p. cm.
"A High Tide Press book."
ISBN 0-8362-5205-5 (hd.)
1. Cats —Anecdotes. 2. Animal heroes—Anecdotes. I. Title.
SF445.5.S925   1998
636.8'0092'9—dc21
97-46888   CIP

ATTENTION: SCHOOLS AND BUSINESSES
Andrews McMeel books are available at quantity discounts
with bulk purchase for educational, business, or sales promotional use. For information
write to: Special Sales Department,
Andrews McMeel Publishing,
4520 Main Street, Kansas City, Missouri 64111.

If man could be crossed with a cat,

it would improve man,

but would deteriorate the cat.

Mark Twain (1835 - 1910)

For My Mother —
For introducing me to the love of these
extraordinary creatures,
and for putting up with me all these years.

CONTENTS

I

WHAT MAKES A HERO?

HEROES ARE THE GENERALS who lead the uphill charge, and the nurses who hold the hands of dying soldiers. They're the people who lay down their lives for their brothers, and the enlightened sages who forego the pleasures of nirvana to liberate all beings from the wheel of suffering. In some stories, they're the knights who slay wicked dragons, while in others, they're the dragons who slay the wicked knights. And in a few, admittedly rare examples, they're the damsels waiting patiently on the sidelines for the others to stop fighting so they can all get on with their lives. In other words, heroes are born of a wide array of circumstances, and arrive on the scene in many shapes and sizes.

Which brings us to the subject at hand.

Hero *What?*

OUTSIDE A SELECT CIRCLE of initiates, the idea of heroic cats will likely seem far-fetched—perhaps even fanatical. After all, in most accounts of interspecies derring-do, canines have traditionally played the starring role. Cats, by contrast, have enjoyed a decidedly less noble reputation. The qualities most commonly associated with the feline species include selfishness, indolence, cunning, and a tendency toward pique. According to popular opinion, cats extend themselves only insofar as they see an opportunity for a meal or fear the loss thereof.

Yet cats entered the story of human society through a chivalrous action hitherto unmatched by any canine. The scene was ancient Egypt, where grand-scale agriculture led to an unanticipated infestation of rats. One supposes even early farmers knew that stored grain would attract rodents. Somewhat less difficult to envision, perhaps, was the scope of the problem once production grew to accommodate an urban population. Instead of a mere score of rats sneaking in and out of the humble neighborhood corn bin, hundreds of thousands of creatures began to gorge themselves in the world's first grain silos.

The fainthearted may not wish to ponder the size of a truly well-fed rat. The creatures who plundered Egypt's granaries weren't by any stretch of the imagination adorable little whiskered things. They were more likely three-foot-long,

Towser, hero mouser

twenty-pound monsters armed with sharp claws and teeth, voracious appetites, no manners, and even fewer scruples. Now, imagine several hundred thousand such creatures slithering through heaps of grain fouled with droppings, rotting carcasses, and so forth. The idea might reasonably put one off one's feed. Add a remarkable rate of reproduction to the equation, and Egypt's dilemma becomes even plainer.

Enter *Felis Lybia, a* small breed of wildcat. Lured by the prospect of countless obese rodents lolling about the local grain silo, *Felis Lybia* slipped from the wilderness into civilized zones around 1600 B.C. Softly and slowly on velvet paws, they made short work of the lazier specimens. Were nature not infinitely resourceful, the rat population might easily have been wiped out by the stronger, more patient, and rather more hungry cats. As any armchair biologist can tell you, when the slow and the weak members of a species are winnowed away, the survivors breed with one another to produce a more refined class of beings. Thus, over the next few generations, rats became stronger and smarter—and *Felis Lybia* became a permanent partner in Egypt's struggle against the devouring rat.

Despite the many advances designed by the human race over the past several thousand years, few seem to have improved dramatically on nature's own version of the mousetrap. The Glenturret distillery in Scotland, for example, still relies on cats to perform the difficult task of stalking, catching, and eliminating rats from its treasured store of grains. One of the distillery's most skillful champions—a female tortoiseshell named Towser—managed to rid the distillery of an astonishing 28,899 mice by the time of her death in 1987. For her truly prodigious feats of mousery, Towser was awarded a prominent mention in the *Guinness Book of World Records.*

Finding the "House" in the "Housecat"

T HOUGH RELIEVED of the unpleasantness associated with a thriving rodent population, the earliest beneficiaries of feline prowess still had one small problem. *Felis Lybia* was no less apt than his allotted victim to enjoy a dainty morsel of human flesh now and again—particularly if threatened. In order to exert some control over their feline partners, the Egyptians began the difficult process of domestication. Eventually, domesticated cats extended a certain possessiveness over their new abodes in town and country. Over time, *Felis Lybia* became an unwelcome guest at the table of a tamer breed of rat-catcher, *Felis catus.*

It may be argued, of course, that the cats of ancient Egypt acted out of purely selfish motives rather than any altruistic intent. Hunger is unquestionably a superb incitement. Nevertheless, the Egyptians apparently felt such gratitude toward *Felis Lybia* that they elevated the entire species to a semidivine status. A cat-headed god, the wise and powerful Bastet, appeared in the Egyptian pantheon at roughly the same time the Egyptian legal system imposed death on anyone found injuring or killing a cat. The same sentence was carried out even against those attempting to smuggle a cat out of Egypt—hardly the kind of prohibition imposed on an animal considered merely useful.

It would seem that cats were regarded as deliverers and protectors, at least among the Egyptians. Cats themselves have kept silent on that point. One can hardly blame them for their reticence, since human gratitude is often expressed in bizarre ways. For example, sarcophagi and other funerary devices specifically designed for cats have been discovered among the tombs of ancient Egypt, further witness to the esteem in which these animals were held. Recent findings, however, suggest that at least some of the honored dead may have been laid unwillingly to rest. X-ray analysis shows that an alarming number of mummified cats actually perished as a result of mysteriously broken necks.

The Benefits of Anonymity

W ERE THE CATS of three thousand years ago simply clumsier than the cats of today? Possible, but not likely. A more plausible explanation can be found in the ancient Egyptian belief that one's most cherished belongings could accompany one to the underworld after death—a comfort, no doubt, if one were the person dying; for close relations and cherished pets the prospect may have seemed a bit more controversial.

DORIS STRAUS

It's no wonder that cats tend to shy away from advertising their accomplishments. Contemporary society continues to demonstrate a singular barbarity toward those it supposedly honors. Every day across the world, thousands of cats (to say nothing of man's supposed best friend, the tender canine) are put to sleep. From a certain point of view, obscurity may seem preferable to the spotlight of human affection.

Still, many cats insist on extending themselves on behalf of the dull, flabby creatures who imagine themselves rulers of the earth. For their troubles, cats sometimes have their picture taken or receive a medal or citation at a public ceremony—which is as often as not an ordeal in itself. Fame is no reward for valor, and Boots couldn't care less whether his name is spelled right in the evening paper. One suspects that the true motive behind the acts of gallantry and heroism described here and elsewhere is far more simple.

Anyone who has experienced some form of direct communication with a member of another species knows what a miracle is. When two creatures can't possibly understand each other, yet both know precisely what the other is thinking, all limitations drop away. For those fortunate enough to have connected with a cat in such a way—or witnessed the profound compassion and courage these creatures can display—may the present volume strengthen your memories. For the rest, may it serve as a chance to examine a very special variety of heroism.

2

MOTHER LOVE: BIOLOGY OR ETHICS?

WHY DO SOME CREATURES give freely of themselves while others cannot? Worker bees exert themselves intensely for the good of the hive for six weeks, until they quite literally drop dead. By contrast, the wife of an American president once publicly suggested that the country would be far better off if everyone gave as little as fifteen minutes a day to a worthy cause. No one took her seriously—least of all her husband, who left office in some disgrace.

The complexities of animal behavior have captured the imagination of thinking persons at least since the days of Plato and Aristotle. Eventually, two different ideas about animal behavior evolved. One school of thought held that all animal activity was learned. During the late nineteenth century, a Russian scientist by the name of Ivan Pavlov demonstrated that dogs could learn to associate certain irrelevant cues with food. After consistently ringing a bell each time he served up a hearty bowl of kibble, Pavlov discovered that his dogs eventually began to salivate simply upon hearing the bell.

The other school held that behavior rises almost entirely from instinct. Faced for the first time with the long, narrow bill of its parent, for example, a baby herring gull will unerringly peck on the red spot at the tip of the beak, provoking the parent to regurgitate breakfast. Alas, the poor chick will respond in the same fashion to a knitting needle painted with a red spot, upon which no amount of pecking will induce disgorgement.

Most sensible people, however, agree that animal behavior probably stems from both instinct and training. The real motives behind any action will probably always retain a mysterious aspect. We may never know, for example, if Pavlov's dogs—goaded by an instinctive urge to be liked—salivated in response to certain associations with the dinner bell, or merely in order to please the kind, if somewhat barmy, Russian doctor.

Many species set aside issues of individual convenience in order to aid close family members. Worker bees represent an extreme expression of this worthy social program, commonly referred to as "kin selection." A somewhat more conventional picture may be drawn by the case of male lions, who are known to assume responsibility for a deceased or wounded brother's family. Female lions, meanwhile, frequently hunt in groups comprised of sisters, mothers, cousins, and aunts (of both the maiden and married variety), and typically share the spoils in the fashion of a large family picnic.

Oddly enough, though humans seem only too happy to publicize similar programs, the need to advertise family ideals at all suggests that kin selection may be at odds with more potent motivations. It would appear that humans infinitely prefer *debating* paternal obligations to actually *fulfilling* them. Exceptions to the norm continue to surprise and delight us, of course. Nevertheless, a casual review of television talk shows may cause one to wonder how many of the guests would rather blubber away on national television than plunge headlong into a burning building for the sake of a child.

Frankly, She Gave
a Damn

I N MANY WAYS, Brooklyn has become synony-
mous with a kind of colorful, gutsy integrity—
commonly referred to as *chutzpah.* It's been home to a wide variety of immigrant cultures, a legendary baseball team, a number of colorful gangsters, and its share of brilliant artists. On
March 29, 1996, a comparatively unknown neighborhood in
the northeast corner of Brooklyn—known as East New
York—briefly commanded the world's spotlight.

While the rest of the city patiently endured the mis-
erable cold typical of early spring, blistering heat blasted
Livonia Street after an abandoned vacant auto shop caught
fire. Black smoke billowed from broken windows and flames
knifed through the roof. The red lights of the fire engines
swirled as plumes of water arched through the sky.

Firefighters had just about succeeded in extinguishing
the blaze when David Giannelli, a seventeen-year veteran of
Ladder Company 17, heard the faint sound of meowing near
the side of the ruined building. Stepping carefully through the
acrid smoke, Giannelli discovered two four-week-old kittens
huddled together outside the building. Almost immediately,
three more were discovered across the street. Nearby, badly
burned, lay the mother, who had succeeded in rescuing her kittens from the burning garage.

Even those familiar with the physiology of cats may not fully comprehend the mother's uncommon love and determination. At least from a cat's point of view, transporting kittens is hardly a matter of scooping two or three at a time in one's arms and dashing out the door. It's a slow, aggravating process of seizing one kitten at a time by the scruff of the neck and carrying it from place to place. Even under the best conditions, carrying in one's jaws a living creature that weighs at least as much as one's entire head makes for a difficult journey. Add rank black smoke, blistering heat, and the kittens' own sense of urgency and terror to the scene, and the mere thought of repeating it five times until each of one's babies is carried alive from a steadily escalating inferno becomes nearly unimaginable.

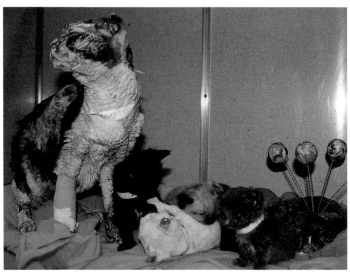

MARY BLOOM

Giannelli carefully gathered mother and kittens into a box. Even then, scorched and blistered, the calico did not fail in her concern. "Though her eyes were swollen shut and her paws burned," he told reporters, "the cat made a head count of her young ones, touching each kitten with her nose to make sure they were all there."

Giannelli brought the cats to the North Shore Animal League in Port Washington, Long Island. The largest pet adoption agency in the world, the NSAL is equipped with a state-of-the-art veterinary hospital and emergency medical service headed by Dr. Bonnie Brown. Ten years earlier, Giannelli had brought a dog suffering extensive burns to the North Shore Animal League, and their success in restoring the dog's health convinced him that the League was the right place to bring the cats.

MARY BLOOM

Mother and babies were immediately treated for burns, smoke inhalation, and related injuries, and placed in an intensive-care oxygen chamber—a large cage equipped with temperature and humidity controls. The mother cat soon became known as Scarlett, partly because of the red patches that could be seen through her burned fur, and partly in honor of the screen heroine who saved Melanie and her newborn son from the flames that felled Atlanta during the Civil War.

Scarlett's eyelids were blistered shut as a result of her repeated forays into the burning garage. Despite the pain, she maintained a vigilant guard over her brood, relinquishing them from her scorched paws only when members of Dr. Brown's dedicated staff examined them. Of the five kittens rescued, only one did not survive the trauma; and though Scarlett eventually regained her sight, doctors at NSAL surgically replaced her left eyelid.

Meanwhile, Scarlett's fierce display of motherly love made headlines around the world. Day after day, calls poured in from as far away as South Africa, the Netherlands, and Japan. Many people, touched by Scarlett's courage, called to offer her and her family a home. Others simply wanted to ask about their welfare. As the survivors recuperated, the staff of the NSAL began to consider the most appropriate response to the thousands of adoption offers they'd received. Two of the kittens, Samsara and Tanuki, were eventually placed in a home in Port Washington, where NSAL is located. Oreo and Smokey—named for the color of their fur—were given a home in nearby Miller Place, New York.

Scarlett herself has returned to Brooklyn, taking up residence in the home of a writer whose previous cat had passed away at the ripe old age of twenty-one. Though she requires medicated eye cream three times a day, she is otherwise quite fit. Her coat is now thick and glossy, and she weighs a healthy fifteen pounds. If she takes any pride in the heroic rescue that made her an international celebrity, she seems to have kept it in perspective. The few photographs she has allowed show a pert, slightly shy young feline, whose face expresses a timely wisdom for a shallow age: Fame is fleeting, but true love lasts forever.

Trial by Water

T HE BIRTH OF KITTENS, if expected, can be a miraculous event. Of course, accidents happen even in the best of families, many of whom take the embarrassment and other social consequences in stride and steadfastly provide for the erring mother and her innocent newborns. Should they be unable to keep or find homes for Bootsie's offspring on their own, humans gifted with a fully functioning moral sense usually take the kittens to a local shelter or adoption agency. Naturally, they will also take steps to ensure that Bootsie doesn't fall from grace in the future.

A number of humans seem to reach adulthood without developing what, for lack of a better term, may be called a heart. All would be well if such unfortunate creatures simply stayed home dribbling on the back porch. Unfortunately, many do not. When confronted with an unexpected litter of kittens, such morally crippled individuals often respond in despicable ways. We'll never know the name of the heartless person who, in the early spring of 1970, wrapped an American Shorthair and her kittens in a burlap bag and tossed them from a one-lane bridge into the icy water below. For Princess and her kittens, surviving the plunge into Wheeling Creek, a shallow tributary of the Ohio River, was only the beginning of a life-and-death struggle.

1970

The creek was still fairly shallow at that time of year, and instead of sinking, the bag lodged against a collection of twigs, mud, and rotted leaves projecting from the bank. Frigid water slowly began to fill the sack. Spurred by the high-pitched cries of her kittens, the frantic mother began ripping at the burlap with her claws and teeth. She may have been aided by a small preexisting hole, or perhaps the water helped weaken the burlap fibers. With great effort, however, she managed to free herself and tumble into the icy creek.

Most cats regard water the same way some humans regard great, hairy spiders: Every gland, every nervous fiber compels them to flee. So the choice between running away and confronting terrific personal horror for the sake of others can be reasonably judged to prove one's mettle. Standing in the shallow waters, Princess thrust her head into the bag. She began by extracting a kitten by the scruff of the neck and carrying it to the bank, then crawled back into the water to save the next.

HERO CATS

In her haste, she wouldn't have stopped to consider the possibility that the bag—gradually lightened of its burden—would begin to drift. We can only imagine her horror as she turned from depositing the third of her five kittens safely on the bank, and watched the two still trapped in the bag begin to float out of reach. She stepped further out, slipping on the mud, as one of the two tiny creatures poked its wet face out of the hole in the bag and began to cry. Naturally, she called back to her little one, offering what solace she could.

Though not herself an avid reader, from that morning on Princess may well have regarded home newspaper delivery as a blessing. For in the moment of her greatest need, eleven-year-old Bobby Stando of Fairpoint, Ohio, was just completing his morning paper route. As he approached the bridge, he couldn't help but hear the cries of pain and fear below. He dropped his bike and slid down the bank in time to see Princess make a desperate lunge for the burlap bag.

Without thinking about the hell he might catch from his mother for getting wet and dirty, he splashed into the creek, grabbing the bag in one hand and Princess in the other, and carried them both to shore.

Bobby scooped mother and kittens into the canvas sack in which he normally carried his newspapers, and carefully transferred the little family to the front basket of his bicycle. As he mounted the bike and prepared to ride homeward, he wondered if the mother might jump out and run away.

"She looked so scared," he recalled more then twenty years later. "I can still see those big eyes staring at me, and the wet fur stuck to her face. But as soon as I started pedaling, the kittens started crying, and she forgot all about me. She started dealing with her babies, licking them, trying to pull them close with her paws. I tried not to hit any bumps, but every time I did, she'd look up at me again. Not accusing, but as if she was trying to tell me it was all right and not to worry, that she trusted me and knew I was doing the best I could."

Miraculously, Princess and four of her five kittens survived the ordeal. Sadly, the fifth —who'd become caught in the bottom of the burlap bag as it floated away—drowned before Bobby managed to retrieve the bundle from the stream.

When Bobby arrived home, his mother was initially reluctant to let him bring the soaking, muddy cats any further than the basement. However, she did help him build a nest for them, gathering a cardboard box and some clean rags, fresh from the dryer. But as she listened to Bobby's story of

Princess's courage and watched the tiny creatures clinging desperately to their mother, Carol Stando decided they'd had a hard enough life. She carried the box herself up to the kitchen. Later that afternoon, she and Bobby buried the lone casualty, a little female they decided to call Angel, in the backyard.

Over the next few weeks, the four remaining kittens—Napoleon, Jack, Beauty, and Dart—grew bigger and stronger. Soon, the Stando family realized that they couldn't provide five adult cats with the care and attention they needed, and agreed that the best solution would be to find homes for the kittens.

One by one, the kittens departed, and Bobby made sure they all said good-bye to their mother before they left. As though she knew she was seeing her children for the last time, Princess gave each a final, hearty scrub between the ears, and afterward stood on the windowsill to watch her little one disappear down the street. Princess herself stayed with the Stando family until her death at age fifteen, at which time she was buried in the backyard, right beside her littlest Angel.

Adventures in Babysitting

A NUMBER OF COMPELLING reasons underlie the feline species' efforts to project an independent image. One has only to observe the unfortunate example of the *other* popular species of domesticated animal to grasp the sad consequences of familiarity. To be sure, some comfort may be derived from gaining a reputation as man's best friend. Yet in return, one must put up with certain quasi-derogatory remarks. How often, for instance, do humans hurl insults such as "low-down, dirty cat" or "cat-and-pony show"?

Nonetheless, the effort to maintain one's dignity is fraught with risks. How easily one becomes the target of slander! Over the centuries, old wives have done the most damage to the feline reputation. The worst of the vile rumors they've spread involves the fantastic notion that cats can suck the life breath from a sleeping infant. The old wife who came up with such an outlandish idea obviously never gave a thought to anatomy and physiology. The feline breathing apparatus is simply not powerful enough to function as a vacuum cleaner.

The idea may have its roots in a misguided attempt to explain the somewhat unusual instances when cats have been caught in the rather undignified activity of breathing through their mouths. Cats typically inhale through their noses except when engaging a highly specialized organ at the back of the throat known as Jacobsen's organ. The organ is a kind of hybrid structure capable of recording smells and tastes at the same time. Cats breathing with their mouths open are literally "tasting" the air in order to specifically catalogue a strange new scent.

Under no circumstances can the Jacobsen's organ serve to draw air from another creature—certainly not one equipped with as lusty a pair of lungs as the typical human infant. Neither do cats accidentally smother human infants by mistaking them for nice, warm pillows. As a rule, pillows don't slobber, urinate, bite, or twist around of their own accord— all conditions a cat would find most uncomfortable. More significantly, no medical establishment has ever recorded a single cat-related infant fatality.

Nevertheless, the climate of fear generated by old wives' tales caused Mary Peckroad to feel some misgivings about the way her five-year-old cat, Mr. Meow, might respond when baby Samantha was brought home from the hospital.

"I'd heard that cats can feel abandoned when a baby is brought into the household," the Fort Collins, Colorado, resident explained. "I was worried that Mr. Meow might scratch or bite Sam out of jealousy."

Wisely, the Peckroads took care to give Mr. Meow a bit of extra attention before Samantha was born. They also let him investigate all the changes being made around the house in preparation for the baby's arrival. "We didn't let the cat choose the color scheme or anything like that," joked Tom Peckroad, "but we did let him wander in and out of the baby's room while we painted and arranged the furniture. We wanted to make sure he knew he was welcome."

When Sam came home, Mr. Meow was clearly fascinated with the new arrival. According to Mary, "He'd take up a perch while I fed or changed her, as though he were standing guard. When I rocked the baby, he'd lie on the arm of the sofa, watching. Once or

twice, he even put his paw on the arm of the rocker, as if he thought I was rocking too fast. His seriousness around Sam was truly comical."

A few months after Samantha was born, Mary Peckroad finally got around to hanging the mobile of hand-carved wooden stars she'd received at her baby shower. Suspended neatly over Sam's crib, the gift perfectly suited the room, which had been decorated with a border of stenciled stars and moons. A few days later, while Samantha was napping, Mary took the opportunity to straighten up the house.

"All of a sudden, I heard the strangest yowling coming down the hall," she remembered. "I thought at first that

Mr. Meow was just looking for one of his toys. We'd started putting his things out of reach because Sam was starting to crawl around, and we didn't want her putting little rubber balls and catnip mice in her mouth. I called for Mr. Meow a couple of times, but he wouldn't come."

Instead, the yowling grew more frantic, and Mary thought perhaps Mr. Meow had gotten stuck somewhere. As she hurried down the hall, she realized the sounds were coming from the baby's room, and the old wives' tales came back to haunt her. She imagined Mr. Meow had finally had his fill of Sam, and was trying to drive her away.

When she ran into the room, however, Mary immediately spotted the cat on a dresser peering anxiously into the crib. He turned and uttered a piercing cry that brought her rushing to the side of the crib—where she saw, to her horror, that the mobile had fallen into the crib, and baby Sam had gotten tangled up in the cords. More frightening still, one of the cords was wrapped tightly around the child's neck.

"Sam was turning blue," Mary recalled later on. "If I hadn't gotten there when I did, I don't even want to think about what might have happened."

She cut the strings away, and rushed Sam to the emergency room, where a pediatrician pronounced her a healthy—and very lucky—little girl.

"We're incredibly grateful to Mr. Meow," Mary said. "If he weren't standing guard that day, we could so easily have lost our little girl. I just hope all our babysitters will take their job as seriously as Mr. Meow."

Tom Peckroad heartily seconded his wife's sentiments—adding only that he doubted other babysitters will be satisfied with a scratch behind the ears and a few extra helpings of ground liver and chicken.

A CAT MAY LOOK AT A KING

THROUGHOUT HISTORY, quite a number of world rulers were noted for their affinity for cats, including Louis XV, Queen Victoria, Winston Churchill, and Abraham Lincoln. None, however, seem to have so consciously joined their destiny to the life of a beloved pet as King Charles I of England. Charles owned a black cat, which at the time was considered a sign of extreme good fortune in many quarters of the world. Not surprisingly, then, the king's concern for the cat's welfare was fairly intense, and a guard was assigned to ensure its protection and well-being.

Alas, Charles was a clumsy ruler whose political ineptitude ultimately led to several years of civil war. During his numerous attempts to put down rebellions in various unpleasant areas of the country, his beloved cat fell ill. The very day after the unfortunate animal departed for the nether shore, Charles was captured by enemy troops. He was proclaimed a tyrant and murderer, and publicly beheaded. Given this tragic turn of fate, Charles may have felt entirely justified in his belief in the protective power of black cats. We will never know for sure how the cat felt about the king—though it's probably safe to say that thereby hangs a tale!

3

GRACE UNDER FIRE: CATS IN WARTIME

OR THOUSANDS OF YEARS, the battlefield has served as the great proving ground of the heroic temper. Defenders always have an easier time justifying their actions than invaders, of course. Even in more recent times, abstract values such as faith, freedom, or a way of life could be counted on to provide the grounds for heroic action. And where an exact motive was unclear, one could always be guided by the idea that the lives of one's fellow soldiers rested on one's own shoulders.

The larger share of military honors has gone to men—who also happen to have initiated most of the conflicts for which such prizes are regularly awarded. It should come as

no surprise, then, that women and children have received somewhat less recognition. However, during World War II, a rare pocket of enlightened thinkers created a special award for animals who served with exceptional bravery either in the armed services or civil defense units. The award, known as the Dickin Medal, was established by Maria Dickin, founder of the People's Dispensary for Sick Animals.

Mrs. Dickin created the People's Dispensary in 1917 as a means of providing free veterinary treatment to pet owners who could not otherwise obtain medical care for their sick and injured animals. During World War II, the PDSA rescued and treated more than a quarter million animals injured during bombing raids. At the same time, the organization also formed the Allied Forces Mascot Club, whose two thousand–strong membership consisted exclusively of animals officially connected to the armed services or civil defense units.

As sponsor of the Dickin Medal, the Mascot Club recognized distinguished wartime services offered by thirty-one carrier pigeons, eighteen dogs, and three horses. Only one cat ever received the award—a commendable feline named Simon, who served with distinction on a ship trapped on the banks of the Yangtze River.

After reviewing the record, one might be tempted to think that the medal's sponsors maintained some type of discriminatory policy toward cats. Closer inspection, however, indicates a more likely explanation. Simon's award represented the only such commendation extended to a member of the Royal Navy. Since cats were traditionally associated with that particular branch of the armed services, it's far more reasonable to assume that jealousy among various factions of the armed services kept the coveted honor from being awarded to other deserving felines.

The Yangtze Incident

SIMON WAS ENGAGED IN THE FINE ART of chasing small, useless objects across the floor when Captain Bernard Skinner of HMS *Amethyst* entered an armaments supply store on Stonecutter's Island, Hong Kong. It was early spring, 1948. The supply clerk noticed Captain Skinner watching the eight-month-old kitten and asked if the *Amethyst* might need the services of a mouser.

Captain Skinner nodded. Even in the twentieth century, a three hundred-foot warship like the *Amethyst* was prone to infestations of rats, mice, and other unsavory creatures. The clerk lifted Simon from the floor and transferred him to the captain's arms. He assured Captain Skinner that the lithe, little black-and-white came from a long line of distinguished ship's cats, and would no doubt serve the *Amethyst* extremely well. At the captain's request, the clerk etched Simon's name and the name of the ship on a small metal tag, which he fastened around the cat's neck with a leather collar.

For the next year, Simon led a fairly cozy, if predictable, existence. A special favorite of Captain Skinner, Simon slept in the captain's cabin and ate regularly in the officer's mess. In between forays through the galley and stores, he fraternized with officers and ordinary seamen alike, becoming a familiar and largely comforting presence.

In April 1949, the *Amethyst* sailed up the Yangtze River from Shanghai on a mission to relieve the British warship *Consort*, which had been guarding the British Embassy further upriver, in Nanking. The south side of the Yangtze was controlled by Chinese Nationalist forces; the north side, by Communist troops. If the Nationalists refused to surrender to the stronger Communist forces by midnight on April 20, the truce between the two armies would expire, and the British Embassy staff would need to be evacuated.

Night traffic on the Yangtze was forbidden, so the *Amethyst* put up anchor at Kiangyin on the evening of April 19. In the early hours of April 20, Captain Skinner ordered the crew to continue on to Nanking. A few hours later, the Communist forces mistook the frigate for a Nationalist warship and opened fire. Shells crashed into the ship, tearing holes in the sides and sending torrents of exploding metal through the air. Captain Skinner, along with several members of the crew, perished in the attack.

Simon himself was singed by the explosions and wounded by several pieces of shrapnel, and several days passed before he crawled out from under Captain Skinner's bunk. The ship's surgeon cleaned and dressed his wounds and treated him for dehydration. After several days, he recovered sufficiently to resume his active duties—more necessary than ever now that the ship had become a virtual prisoner of war.

Apparently, the Communist forces refused to release the *Amethyst* until the new commander, Captain John Kerans, publicly declared that the British had started the attack by firing on the Communist camp. Such an admission would have significantly impaired any hope of peacefully resolving the situation now commonly referred to as the Cold War. Caught up in a sensitive diplomatic struggle, the *Amethyst's* crew suffered uncertainty in an unending chain of sweltering days and nights. Except for the highest members of British military establishment, no one knew of the ship's plight. As far as the outside world knew, the *Amethyst* had simply dropped out of sight.

The real significance of a mouser aboard ship may easily be lost on those who've never served at sea. Even under the best of conditions, vermin never seem to exhaust the possibilities of slipping aboard under cover of darkness or stowing away in supply boxes and other freight shipments. Unchecked, rats and mice will brazenly feast on food stores and chew through fabrics, cables, and other necessary items. They also play host to a fairly loathsome group of parasites that can transfer a broad range of nasty diseases to unsuspecting sailors.

On the *Amethyst*, days passed slowly while surviving crew members struggled to repair damage from the shelling. Temperatures climbed to over 110 degrees and stores began to dwindle. By mid-July, the crew had been reduced to half rations. Were it not for Simon's persistence, the rats climbing aboard ship from the banks of the river could have eroded supplies even further. According to a report printed weeks later in the London *Daily Telegraph*, Simon bagged at least one rat a day.

Simon made a particularly spectacular kill near the end of April, while still recovering from his wounds. As one of the ship's chief officers watched, he stalked and pounced on an enormous black rat, which the crew had nicknamed Mao Tse Tung. With a sharp bite to neck, Simon sent Mao Tse Tung winging into his next incarnation. The officer carried both Simon and the rat to the deck, where the former was cheered and the latter flung unceremoniously overboard.

Simon might easily have abandoned ship on several occasions. Yet as days passed into weeks, he chose to stay on, ridding the *Amethyst* of vermin and performing the no less vital function of maintaining morale. When not greeting the sailors above decks, or contributing a certain esprit du corps by showing off his daily kill, Simon regularly visited the ship's hospital, where men wounded in the Communist attack lay recovering.

One patient in particular benefited from Simon's hospital visits. Seaman Mark Allen, a boy of only sixteen, had lost both his legs during the shelling. Suffering from acute pain and depression, the boy refused to speak or eat. When the ship's doctor introduced Simon, Mark patted the cat's back and smiled for the first time in days. The next time Simon visited, he settled down on Mark's stomach, staring with bright green eyes into the boy's face. Slowly, as he stroked the cat's singed fur, Mark began to cry. Through whatever mysterious, sympathetic conjunction, Simon had managed to break through the wall the boy had built up around himself.

The ship's doctor quickly ordered a bowl of soup from the galley, and while Simon sat watching by his side, Mark ate for the first time in more than a week. From then on, Simon visited every day, rubbing against his new friend, supervising his meals, and gratefully allowing the young sailor to brush his singed, dirty coat.

At the end of July, a typhoon tore up the Yangtze River. Though rain lashed the decks, and hurricane-force winds rocked the boat, Simon still refused to relinquish his duties. When the storm passed, he resumed his hospital visits and his daily rounds amid the ship's dwindling stores. More than one officer took pride in the fact that a cat accustomed to a life of comparative luxury as the captain's favorite should prove his mettle under difficult conditions when the need arose.

As he examined the ship in the aftermath of the storm, Captain Kerans realized that he and his men would be reduced to quarter rations in a matter of days. Disinfectant and other medical supplies were also running out. Worse, the ship's generators were burning two tons of fuel a day. With only fifty-five tons in reserve, it was only a matter of days before the *Amethyst* would lack the means to turn and proceed downriver toward Shanghai. The ship would be permanently imprisoned on the Yangtze.

Faced with such a grim possibility, Captain Kerans decided to chance a 120-mile run downriver. On the night of July 30, under cover of a cloudy sky, the *Amethyst* stealthily turned and headed toward Shanghai. Throughout the daring escape, Simon remained staunchly at Captain Kerans's side on the bridge. The frigate was fired on several times by Communist forces hidden along the bank of the river, but she escaped further damage. Shortly after dawn, the *Amethyst* rejoined the British fleet with barely nine tons of fuel left in her tanks.

On August 1, Captain Kerans assembled the crew on deck for a ceremony awarding Simon with a special *Amethyst* campaign ribbon for steadfastly performing his duties while recovering from his own wounds—and in particular for ridding the ship of the monstrous Mao Tse Tung. After the ceremony, Captain Kerans decided to nominate Simon for a Dickin Medal.

Word of the *Amethyst*'s spectacular dash to freedom traveled quickly—and with it, the tale of Simon's devotion, which had done so much to bolster the morale of his fellow crew members. In short order, the PDSA Allied Forces Mascot Club decided unanimously to award Simon the Dickin Medal. As the *Amethyst* made its way back to London, press coverage and correspondence generated by Simon's gallantry compelled Captain Kerans to appoint a ship's officer to oversee "cat affairs" and answer Simon's mail.

The *Amethyst* arrived in Plymouth on November 1, 1949. Even today, British law insists that any cat entering the country must spend six months in quarantine. No exceptions seem to be allowed for war heroes. Accordingly, the Lord Mayor of London, Maria Dickin, and several other dignitaries decided to visit Simon in the quarantine kennels in

Hackbridge, Surrey, to present him with his award. Meanwhile, gifts and messages arrived in a steady stream. A group of cats in Chelsea, for example, sent the following poem—the heroic tone of which seems to reflect their devotion toward Victorian favorites such as Tennyson and Gerard Manley Hopkins:

> *Oh Simon of the* Amethyst,
>
> *Stout member of her crew,*
>
> *We fill our saucers high with milk*
>
> *And drink a health to you . . .*

One must remember that Simon was born and raised in a tropical climate, and London's cold climate could hardly be considered healthy for a cat suffering shrapnel wounds or shell shock. Though personally cared for by quarantine officials, Simon became ill within a month of his arrival. On November 28, several days before the planned presentation ceremony, a worker at the kennel noticed that the young hero—normally so alert and inquisitive—seemed listless.

A veterinarian from the Royal College of Veterinary Surgeons was summoned. After examining Simon, the doctor concluded that the little cat, whose constitution had been weakened by his wounds and exposure to extreme heat, had contracted an intestinal virus. The doctor administered some intravenous medication, and left some tablets along with instructions. Joyce Pallack of the PDSA remained by Simon's side through the rest of the day. As night fell, she ran her hand comfortingly across the glossy black and white fur, and realized that the little cat was no longer breathing. Simon, hero of the *Amethyst*, had died.

Though a flood of stories appeared in newspapers and magazines around the world, Simon was buried quietly in the PDSA cemetery in Ilford, Essex. His cotton-lined coffin was covered with a Union Jack and lowered into a grave marked by a temporary headstone. Truckloads of flowers sent by admirers around the world were handsomely arranged around the grave.

In Simon's memory, the PDSA sponsored a Memorial Fund to help promote the welfare of animals in seaports, and a special plaque was erected on his behalf at a quiet ceremony in Plymouth. The Admiral of the Fleet presented Simon's Dickin Medal to Captain Kerans, who donated it to the Naval Museum in Portsmouth. The medal was later sold to a private collector in Canada. In 1993, the London auction firm Christie's sold the medal to a film company for 23,000 pounds (about $38,375).

"The Bravest Cat in the World"

T HOUGH CATS CERTAINLY have played their part in a number of great naval battles, few have been tested quite as severely on the home front as a gallant little tabby named Faith. Her youth remains a mystery. Faith was a stray who wandered into the London church of St. Augustine and St. Faith on Watling Street one cold, wet afternoon in 1936. Perhaps she'd been abandoned by her original owners, who, like so many well-intentioned persons during the Depression era, simply lacked the means to care for themselves, much less their cherished dependants.

The church caretaker attempted several times to remove the little tabby from the premises. Her insistence on hearing Mass, however, and her sweet, somewhat shy manner captivated St. Augustine's rector, Reverend Henry Ross. Ross insisted that the cat be allowed to remain, and he even made a bed and litter box available in his room on the third floor of the rectory. Reverend Ross himself chose the name that would make Faith famous as an international symbol of wartime fortitude.

From the day she arrived at St. Augustine, Faith became a model parishioner, attending Mass regularly and welcoming newcomers and longtime church members alike. At

the beginning of each service, she took part in the procession down the aisle, and afterward chose a seat at the very front of the church. When Reverend Ross delivered his sermon, Faith would rise from her pew and curl at his feet—perhaps not so much to keep an eye on the congregation as to inspire wakefulness in those inclined to sleep.

Toward the end of the summer of 1940, her attendance became somewhat irregular—not through any lapse of devotion, but rather as a result of her delicate condition. As August drew to a close, Faith gave birth to a single black and white kitten. Inspired by the new arrival's coloring, the rector and his staff decided to name the little male Panda, after the favorite attraction then on display at the London Zoological Society.

As Hitler's troops marched across Europe, a sense of nervous anticipation settled over England. Food, coal, and other precious commodities had been rationed since the beginning of the year. In May 1940, Holland and Belgium surrendered to the German troops, followed by France in June. In July, the Germans began bombing the British coast, steadily working their way inland to destroy railroads and factories.

Since the feline predictive capabilities have yet to be thoroughly explored, no one can say with any certainty what inspired Faith to bring her kitten to a safer spot inside the rectory. Three days before the great bombing of London, she insisted on carrying Panda by the scruff of the neck from the third floor to a sort of recess or pigeonhole in the basement. Following her down to the basement, Reverend Ross watched them settle into the recess, which was protected in part by stacks of old organ music. Fearing, however, that Faith and her newborn might catch cold in the cellar, the rector carried mother and kitten back to their warm bed beside the fireplace in his room. Faith returned to the cellar three more times before Reverend Ross finally gave in and had her bed and litter box brought down to the basement recess.

Three nights later, on September 8, 1940, the Germans dropped their bombs on the city of London. St. Augustine stood directly in the shadow of St. Paul's cathedral, the principal target of the German bombs. The entire area around the great cathedral erupted in a hellish scene of carnage, twisted metal, and incinerating flames. Reverend Ross was in Westminster at the time of the bombing. The next morning, he hurried back to London to find that St. Augustine had taken a direct hit. A German bomb had pierced the roof of the rectory, and most of the building had collapsed in flames.

Firemen on the scene forbade Reverend Ross from searching the burning debris for Faith and Panda, telling him in no uncertain terms that the cat and her kitten couldn't have survived the bomb. Reverend Ross stood staring hopelessly at the smoking ruins until the firemen were called away to another emergency. The rector then picked his way through the burning remains, calling for Faith.

The basement recess where Faith had chosen to spend the previous three nights was completely covered by rubble. As he neared the spot, however, Reverend Ross heard

Faith answering his cry. He seized an axe that had been left behind by the firemen and chopped through the smoldering timbers and shingles. Faith lay quite still in her cubbyhole, using her own body to shield Panda from the smoke and flames. She watched calmly as Reverend Ross made his way toward the pair.

"Her attitude," he described later, "said unmistakably, 'Why haven't you come to fetch us sooner?' "

With the aid of a fireman, he pulled mother and kitten completely unharmed from the wreckage, only moments before the remaining wall of the rectory collapsed, completely engulfing the recess in flames and smoke. Ross carried his charges into the vestry tower, which was still standing. There, Faith began licking herself and Panda. According to the rector, she paused every once in a while to lift her head and sing "such a song of praise and thanksgiving as I had never heard from her before."

When Panda grew old enough to be separated from his mother, he was given to a nursing home in Herne Hill, where his company cheered patients recovering from devastating illnesses. Meanwhile, as the war dragged on, Faith's example of simple courage and devotion during the bombing became an inspiration to her neighbors and other visitors to the church. In time, Reverend Ross hung her picture in the tower chapel, where services were held until the church was rebuilt. Underneath, he posted an inscription that read in part:

> Our dear little church cat of St. Augustine and St.
> Faith, the bravest cat in the world. On Monday,
> September 9th, 1940, she endured horrors and perils
> beyond the power of words to tell. Shielding her kitten in
> a sort of recess in the house . . . she sat the whole fright-
> ful night of bombing and fire, guarding her little kitten.
> The roofs and masonry exploded, the whole house
> blazed, four floors fell through in front of her. Fire and
> water and ruin all around her. Yet she stayed calm and
> steadfast and waited for help . . .

Gradually, Faith's story began to circulate more widely, appearing in various newspapers and journals. On the fifth anniversary of the terrible night, her picture and a brief recapitulation of the events appeared in the London *Evening News*. Ultimately, the story came to the attention of Maria Dickin, who, together with Dorothea St. Hill Bourne of the Allied Forces' Mascot Club, decided to bestow a special honor on the little tabby.

Because Faith wasn't an official member of the armed services or civil defense, she was ineligible for the Dickin Medal. However, Mrs. Dickin created a special silver medal engraved with the words:

> From the PDSA to Faith of St. Augustine's Watling
> Street, E.C. For steadfast courage in the Battle of
> London, September 9, 1940.

A certificate was also drawn up, recognizing Faith's courage under fire. Faith received both the certificate and the medal on October 12, 1945, during a special service at St. Augustine, attended by Mrs. Dickin and the Archbishop of Canterbury.

The following year, the Greenwich Village Humane League of New York sent another citation for courage, along with the Paddy Reilly Silver Medal of Honor. By all accounts, Faith remained a humble, steadfast parishioner of the newly rebuilt St. Augustine church. Yet even her quiet end on September 28, 1948, made headlines, as newspapers and journals around the world reported the sad news that "The Bravest Cat in the World" had passed away.

The Little Cabbage
of Nancy

THE GERMAN STRATEGY in World War I was to
send a huge force to wipe out the French in the
west, while the rest of the troops and the entire Austro-
Hungarian army smashed the Russians in the east. The plan,
drawn up a good ten years before there was even a war, called
for German troops to swoop through Belgium, completely
surround the surprised French army, and destroy them. It
somehow never occurred to the Germans that the French
might have caught wind of the plan before the war started.

At first, the French gave their longtime foes reason to
believe the plan might succeed. In little more than a month,
the Germans swept through Belgium and pushed their way
into eastern France. The British and French Allies beat a hasty
retreat to the Marne River, and finally stalled the German
advance there on September 9, 1914. Effectively stalemated,
both sides dug a line of trenches that stretched some five hundred miles from Switzerland to the North Sea.

The trenches, dug approximately six to eight feet
deep, were intended to protect troops from bombs, shells, and
machine-gun fire. Most of the action took place in the front
trenches, while cover trenches, immediately behind, provided a
second line of defense. Off-duty troops ate, slept, and enter-

tained themselves in dugouts in a third row of trenches, and supplies, food, and fresh forces were stored in a fourth row. Between the trenches of opposing forces lay an area littered with barbed wire and clearly within firing range, commonly referred to as No Man's Land. Crossing this open area was considered by most to be a rather ill-conceived idea.

In the middle of 1915, a French soldier named Guillaume Luchaire, stationed along the southern line of trenches near the city of Nancy, received word that his cousin had given birth to a son. Ironically, the cousin was married to a German solider who also happened to be stationed outside of Nancy. International marriage was by no means unusual. Heads of state regularly engaged in the practice and no doubt possessed safe and convenient means of communicating across battle zones. The ordinary fellow, however, required somewhat more ingenuity.

We will never know precisely how Guillaume hit upon the idea of using a cat to communicate with his cousin's husband on the other side of No Man's Land. From time to time, of course, cats visited the trenches on either side of the war zone. Some had been displaced from their homes and sought warmth and sustenance in the third and fourth row of trenches. Others were perhaps drawn by the rats attracted to scraps of food and other trench-bound spoils.

An ordinary little kitty by the name of Choux—the French word for "cabbage"—seemed to have proven himself quite adept at slinking through the trenches, stealing food, and other such activities. Perhaps his apparent cleverness made him a special favorite among the French soldiers; or else, conversely, he simply stole one too many sausages. At any rate, *someone* seemed to have suggested to Guillaume that he tie a note and a white flag around the little cat's neck and toss a tasty morsel out into No Man's Land. Where a man would fail, perhaps a cat could succeed in getting the good news across to the other side.

The spectacle of a dirty little cat stepping delicately through a region strewn with barbed wire, shrapnel, and moonlike craters would no doubt have horrified the average person. Fortunately, soldiers on both sides of No Man's Land were more than a little sick of carnage. Instead of gunfire, the sound of German laughter greeted the cat's progress.

As he neared the other side, the Germans tossed bits of food from their firing trench to lure him closer. Only one deranged soldier thought to frighten the little messenger by firing off a shot in his direction (since no other shots followed, however, it is imagined that his comrades prevailed upon him in what is hoped to be a suitably violent fashion). Undaunted, Choux finally arrived at the German trenches, where waiting hands plucked him from the edge and brought him down into the safety of the dugout. The end of his journey across No Man's Land was greeted by cheers from both sides.

Sensibly, Choux decided that one such adventure was enough for any feline and did not volunteer for a return trip. Only at the end of the war did it become clear that his message had been successfully delivered—when the

German soldier told his French wife that only the thought of someday seeing his little son had kept him alive during the darker moments in the trenches. Because the hopes of so many soldiers and their loved ones had been destroyed by the war, it's perhaps even more wonderful that for Guillaume and his family at least one day came to an end not with a bang, but a whisker.

4

SYMPATHETIC VIBRATIONS

CCOUNTS OF ANIMAL compassion are vigorously repudiated by various scientific and spiritual communities, who exhibit a strong attachment to the idea that animals cannot possess noble sentiments. They agree that animals demonstrate many other traits expressed by the so-called higher orders—for example, greed, curiosity, anger, lust, and an inherent distrust of strangers. Even the habit of protecting one's young can be said to reflect a certain vulgar necessity. However, the capacity to help someone for no other reason than because it's the right thing to do seems to be guarded as jealously as Eden. Like the ability to dream, dance, and write bad poetry, compassion remains for many a strictly human possibility.

Questions of motive must necessarily be handled with considerable delicacy. No doubt, any of the events described below may have been set in motion by no more lofty an incentive than the need to fill one's stomach in the customary place at the customary time. Although our scientific and spiritual friends would likely approve the suggestion that a base instinct for survival drives most, if not all, animal activity, one actually advances along such lines at great philosophical peril. For in so doing, one must assume that animals possess a capacity for complex reasoning that approaches *guile.*

In the final analysis, any interpretation of behavior is an exercise in personal choice. If the reader prefers to live in a world inhabited by creatures who merely pretend to be sympathetic in order to obtain a few lumps of stale ground liver, so be it. Until such time as motivation can be proved beyond a shadow of a doubt, however, the alternative view seems far more agreeable.

Drat, the Brat!

AN OBSCURE BRITISH PHILOSOPHER once observed that "a hard beginning maketh a good ending." While such steely optimism goes a long way toward explaining why British philosophers never achieved the same distinction as their poetical cousins, happy endings nevertheless do surprise us from time to time. Surely no one would have imagined that Brat the cat would have risen from such obscure surroundings to a position of heroic prominence.

For his fifteenth birthday, Jose Ybarra of Wheeling, Indiana, hadn't wanted just any old kitten. The cat he wanted would be the one he "couldn't imagine not taking home." Visits to breeders and pet stores proved disheartening, however, until one July afternoon, when a somewhat frowsy black kitten with white markings on her chest popped up in a pet store window. The riddle of karmic connection—like the mystery of love itself—may never be adequately unraveled. Yet the potency of its spell cannot be denied by anyone who has ever experienced it. As the kitten curled up in his arms, Ybarra knew he'd found the companion he'd been looking for.

The pet store owner told Jose and his mother, Karen Hummerich, that the kitten had been found in an abandoned car. One would naturally assume that an orphan thus rescued might be inclined to exhibit a certain degree of humble gratitude upon finding herself in a warm, comfortable home.

After settling into her new digs, however, the kitten began making an undeniable—if amusing—nuisance of herself. She developed a taste for climbing curtains, pouncing on furniture, and nosing after her new companions like the proverbial baby sister. After playfully bopping Karen on the head one day, she earned the nickname by which she's been known ever since: Brat.

Early on, Brat established a habit of looking after any member of the family who showed signs of illness. When

Karen returned from work one March afternoon, she found the cat curled up with Jose, who had come home from school feeling sick to his stomach. That evening, red spots began to appear on Jose's arms and chest, and Karen suspected an attack of the measles. She decided to take her son to the doctor the following morning.

Jose turned Brat out of his room that night so he could sleep in peace. During the early morning hours, Karen Hummerich was awakened by the odd sensation of something wet and scratchy pressing against her eyes: Brat was licking her face in an attempt to wake her. Because feline behavior of this sort can usually be taken as a direct application for food, Karen simply shooed the cat away. Brat, however, persisted, and after succeeding in rousing her mistress from sleep, ran down the hall to Jose's room and began scratching furiously on the door.

As Karen followed Brat down the hall, she began to hear strange, thumping noises emanating from her son's room. "It sounded as if he was rearranging the furniture," she later recalled. Yet nothing could have prepared her for the shock, upon opening the door, of seeing Jose thrashing around unconsciously in the throes of a seizure.

Rushed to a hospital in Glenview, the young man lapsed into a coma. Doctors prepared the family for the worst as they related the grim news that Jose's seizure had been brought on by bacterial meningitis, an often fatal infection of the brain and spinal cord. The boy was transferred to Lutheran General Hospital in Park Ridge, where a team of intensive-care specialists monitored his symptoms. Against all odds, Jose awoke from his coma on the fifth day after his seizure and began responding verbally to family and other visitors. Within weeks, he made a full recovery.

News of Jose's illness spread quickly through the community. As fears of a more widespread infection subsided, the details of his unusual rescue began to circulate. Though the efforts of hospital workers undoubtedly saved Jose's life, Brat's intervention played a crucial role. As Dr. Myron Singer, the Hummerichs' family physician, succinctly explained, "Without the cat, he would have died."

Ultimately, Brat's heroic response came to the attention of both Wheeling village officials and Illinois State Senator Martin Butler. Two months after the early morning rescue, both governing bodies rewarded Brat with a proclamation citing her "ingenuity and persistence" to a medical emergency. The proclamation, presented in a public ceremony on May 12, 1996, represents the first such honor bestowed on a cat in Illinois history.

According to Hummerich, Brat's attitude to the flurry of public attention surrounding her role in Jose's recovery has been characteristically nonchalant. Whatever opinions she may have formed, she has chosen simply to resume a normal life of pouncing, racing, and lying in wait for the unsuspecting ankle or foot to enter her purview. Perhaps our scientific friends will someday discover whether such discretion in the face of publicity is instinctive or learned.

Midnight's Hour

SUPERSTITIONS INVOLVING BLACK CATS have been handed down for thousands of years. Although fishermen's wives frequently kept a black cat at home to prevent disaster from striking their husbands on the open sea, black cats were often seen as witches or demons. Although good luck apparently smiled on the sailor accompanied by a black cat on his way to the pier, the seaman whose path was merely crossed by a wayward feline would probably not need to make any substantial investment in postcards or other letter-writing materials.

It's impossible to trace the exact origin of adverse feline propaganda. Some historians believe that fear of black cats can be traced to early Christian attitudes toward the Egyptian goddess Bastet, who was frequently represented by a handsomely carved black statue. Others have discovered unpleasant hints of antifeline sentiment among the ancient Celts. Regardless of their origin, the entire collection of superstitions has been reduced in modern times to the simple principle that black cats bring bad luck. The case of the Rogers family of Kansas City, however, starkly refutes centuries of negative publicity.

Midnight bravely approached Bernita and Roy Rogers in 1984 at an outdoor barbecue in a field near a friend's home. Charmed, the couple decided to make a home for the tiny stray at the Fort Leavenworth base, where Roy, an army lieutenant colonel, was stationed. Gradually, the black kitten grew to be a proper soldier, mastering the finer points of stalking the enemy—which at the time consisted mainly of squirrels and rabbits—and flushing them from their hiding places. At least for a while, Fort Leavenworth enjoyed greater protection against the most cunning members of the rodent class.

Midnight had been living with the family for nearly two years when their daughter, Stacey, was born several weeks premature. Having lost three children at birth, Bernita and Roy were justifiably attentive to every aspect of Stacey's welfare. Even so, Midnight never showed the slightest sign of jealousy or rejection. "He was curious," Bernita recalls, "content just to sit nearby, looking at Stacey." At the time, no one suspected that the cat was carefully studying the newborn, formulating a precise picture of normal infant behavior.

Six weeks after coming home, Stacey developed what seemed to be a bad cold. Bernita immediately sought medical attention, but the pediatrician who examined Stacey didn't feel the situation warranted too much anxiety. He advised Rogers simply to place a humidifier in Stacey's room, watch, and wait. Bernita followed his instructions; and after putting Stacey down for an afternoon nap, she sat downstairs with her parents, who had come up to Fort Leavenworth for a visit.

She'd hardly settled into her chair before Midnight bounded into the living room and began jumping on her lap and swatting at her legs. Misinterpreting Midnight's signals, Bernita merely shooed the cat away. Within moments of the cat's departure from the living room, however, Bernita and her parents were startled by the sound of an eerie moan coming from the baby monitor in Stacey's bedroom.

Hurrying upstairs to her daughter's room, Rogers found the cat moaning as he perched on the dresser staring intently into the crib where Stacey lay gasping for breath. Only after Bernita took charge of the situation did Midnight stop crying. Stacey was rushed to the hospital, where she was treated for respiratory failure. After spending the night on a respirator, the little girl gradually recovered her strength and fought off the viral infection that had threatened her. Had Midnight not persisted in raising the alarm, Bernita is certain Stacey would have died in her crib.

Eleven years later, Midnight has rather less energy for

such heroic activities. The tiny infant whose life he saved has grown into a happy, healthy schoolgirl. And though he frequently makes nighttime rounds to make sure that his charge is breathing peacefully, by day he prefers to bask in the sun—dreaming, perhaps, of his former battles with the infidel bunny and the conniving squirrel.

Ding, Dong, Bell

THE PAINTED COWBELL Martha Agrelius found at a craft fair in Wyomissing, Pennsylvania, made an attractive addition to her front porch—especially when suspended over the old metal milk can she'd bought a few months earlier. Salem, Martha's cat, seemed to think so, too. Actually, the cat relished the sound it made when he leapt up onto the milk can and began swatting the bell with his paw.

Like Pavlov before him, Salem discovered that certain individuals could be conditioned to respond in a definite, predictable manner to associated stimuli. After a while, he realized he didn't even need to ring the bell to bring sixty-five-year-old

Martha scurrying out to the front porch. All he had to do was stand on the milk can and reach up. On quite a few occasions, neighbors could also be induced to respond to his summons. All in all, the experiment in behavioral conditioning proved enormously satisfying to Salem.

Shortly before Halloween, Martha asked her son-in-law to raise the bell by about twelve inches, firmly out of reach of Salem's paws and the sticky hands of costumed children. The following February, an ice storm visited Wyomissing, coating streets, cars, trees, and sidewalks with a slick, transparent glaze. On the day after the storm, while outside attending to some private business, Salem came upon a disturbing sight. Martha had apparently bundled herself in the odd skins and footwear she customarily adopted in cold weather and ventured out of doors. What Salem could not immediately grasp, however, was why his companion had decided to lie down between the garage door and the front of the automobile.

Approaching cautiously, Salem discerned that all was not well with his companion. Traces of blood painted red webs in the cracked ice around her head. A cursory exploration with his nose and paws revealed Martha's skin to be unusually cold. In response to Salem's ministrations, the old woman opened her eyes and moaned softly. Though awake, however, she seemed incapable of raising herself and moving to a more comfortable resting spot.

Salem came to a cataclysmic decision. Stepping gingerly across the ice, he made his way to the front porch, and leapt onto the swing suspended from the porch roof by a set of rusty chains. For a few awful moments the swing swayed beneath his weight. As the movement gradually ceased, Salem stepped from the swing onto the ice-covered top of the milk can, and positioned himself directly underneath the bell suspended just out of reach. He bunched his powerful leg muscles and shook his head rapidly back and forth, understanding instinctively that the closer an object, the more rapidly it appears to move when the hunter shakes its head.

Gathering his strength, the cat sprang, extending his front paw to swat the bell. He hit the bell squarely, shaking loose a bit of snow and ice and raising a pathetic sort of clunk, and then landed on the icy porch. Because the counting methods of cats and humans differ rather widely in their interpretation, we must rely on Martha's testimony that Salem repeated his efforts nearly a dozen times before vexing a neighbor sufficiently to make him come outside to discover the cause of the repeated clanging.

In good time, Martha was transported to a local hospital, where she was treated for a fractured hip and a slight injury to her left temple. Salem, meanwhile, was rewarded with several bowls of warm milk, a weekly serving of gourmet food, and a handsome plastic ball fitted with a tiny bell, which he can swat around the floor to his heart's content.

Wheezer's Organ

AS MENTIONED in an earlier chapter, cats inhale through their mouths almost exclusively for the purpose of engaging the Jacobsen's organ located at the back of their throats. By contrast, most humans who persist in mouth breathing are either rude or inbred. A few exceptions apply, naturally. When one is suffering from a severe cold or in the grip of an allergic or asthmatic reaction, breathing through the mouth is generally considered acceptable.

When he noticed the puffy kitten in an Atlanta pet store window engaging his Jacobsen's organ, Gary Fielding immediately felt what he called a "sympathetic bond." Gary suffers from nonallergic asthma—a condition that, for no apparent reason, periodically causes a partial constriction of his bronchial passages. As a child, Gary had been given the nickname Wheezer by his grandfather. Accordingly, when he noticed the kitten literally tasting the air as he explored each room of the Atlanta apartment they would share, Gary conferred the same moniker on his new companion.

For Gary, relief from periodic attacks depends on a small plastic hand pump, which dispenses a bronchodilator drug directly into his mouth. Gary has several such pumps around the apartment, in his car, and at work. "In the case of a really severe attack," he explains, "fast access to an inhaler can mean the difference between life and death."

Gary often noticed Wheezer's interest in the events surrounding an attack. Sometimes, the cat would simply sit nearby and stare. Other times, particularly after a severe attack, he might step cautiously closer and pat Gary's cheek with his paw, as if to inquire after his companion's health and satisfy himself that the condition was no longer critical. Once, Gary watched with considerable surprise as Wheezer made his way gingerly onto his lap, stood up on his hind legs, and balanced his front paws on Gary's chin. Leaning close to his face, the cat began breathing tentatively through his mouth—almost as if he were imitating Gary's behavior during the attack. Later, when he relayed the story to Wheezer's veterinarian, the doctor explained that the cat was more than likely attempting to identify the strange scent of the dilator drug on Gary's breath.

It stands as a tribute to the extraordinary sensitivity of the Jacobsen's organ that Wheezer was able to come to his companion's aid. One frightening afternoon, while suffering a particularly sharp attack, Gary was unable to locate his inhaler.

"I was starting to panic," Gary recalled later. "Of course, I have pills I can take to relieve the constriction, but they don't work nearly as fast as the inhaler." After searching frantically through the apartment for several minutes, Gary took a couple of pills and lay down on the bed, trying to breathe calmly and regularly. Caught up in his own fear and acute physical discomfort, he hadn't even noticed Wheezer watching his every move.

"I was lying on the bed with my eyes closed," he explained, "trying to keep the panic from taking over—which isn't necessarily easy when you feel like you're going to suffocate any second—when all of a sudden I heard this clattering in the other room."

Gradually, the clattering noise came closer. Opening his eyes and raising his head a little, Gary was astonished to see that Wheezer had somehow found the missing inhaler, and was intent on batting it across the floor from the living room to the bedroom where Gary lay stricken. Immensely relieved, Gary stood up and retrieved the pump—while Wheezer sat quietly staring up at him. As the medication promptly took effect, Gary took a couple of deep breaths and sat on the floor beside his rescuer.

"I asked him how he knew what I was looking for," Gary said. "He didn't tell me, obviously. He just came up on my lap and put his paw on my mouth—probably as much to make sure that I was breathing all right as to let me know, in some way, that some things should remain a mystery."

Christmas

"THOSE WERE HARD YEARS," Ida Mackenzie recalls. "Even as children, we could see the worry on Mom and Dad's faces, on the faces of our neighbors who ran the farm across the way, on the people we'd see on the street when we went into town. We had food on the table, and a roof over our heads, but we'd hear our parents talking at night—their voices came up through the floor or through the walls—and we understood it was a miracle sometimes that they found a way to make ends meet. They say there's no good times for kids to grow up really, but those were hard times."

She's speaking, of course, about the Great Depression that followed the stock market crash of 1929. By 1932, hundreds of banks had failed, and scores of mills, factories, and other businesses had shut their doors for good. More than 10 million people lost their jobs, and with no livelihood to support workers or consumers, farms and homes across the nation were foreclosed. In spite of emergency farm relief and public works projects, the Great Depression grew steadily worse.

Mackenzie, a Minnesota native, vividly remembers her parents' struggle to keep the modest family farm running. They had to sell off livestock and let go of workers whose families they'd known for two or three generations. Dwindling resources made it absolutely necessary to conserve fuel during the harsh, northwestern winters, when temperatures sometimes dipped twenty or thirty degrees below freezing. At the time, the blessings of a large family outweighed the difficulties.

"My three sisters and I huddled together in one bed to keep warm, and my three brothers did the same in another," Mackenzie explains. "We all pitched in with the chores just to keep the farm running. Things weren't so bad in the summer, but in the winter—how I hated getting out of bed at four in the morning and making my way down to the cold kitchen and then out to the barn."

One frosty morning, shortly after Thanksgiving, twelve-year-old Ida and her eight-year-old brother, Clint, made a remarkable discovery. As they entered the barn to milk the two remaining family cows, a gray tabby cat poked his head out from one of the empty stalls. "Clint wanted to chase the cat away," Ida recalls. "He didn't have much use for cats. He thought they were more sneaky than anything else. Course, he changed his tune pretty quickly once we found out what that cat had dragged in with him, so to speak."

As Ida's brother ran toward the cat, the animal retreated into the stall, but only so far as a small mound of

My cat

Nosy Cat.

hay piled up along the wall. There, the cat not only stood his ground, but to both children's amazement actually emitted a low hiss—or as Ida describes it, a "pathetic little noise, like the last bit of air from a bicycle tire." Ida motioned her brother to stay behind, and she stepped slowly toward the tabby, holding out her hand and making soft, clicking sounds with her tongue. The cat held its ground but allowed her to approach. About a foot from the mound of hay now, Ida at last made out what the cat had been protecting.

"Holy geez," she remembers crying to her brother. "Clint, there's a baby here!"

The infant boy was dressed in pants, shirt, socks, and a little wool hat, and wrapped in a blanket made, as Ida recalls, of "a thin sort of burlap." As she lifted the infant to examine it for signs of life, Ida couldn't help but notice that the blanket was covered with cat hair. Evidently, the cat had slept on top of the boy, warming him like an incubator and virtually guaranteeing his safety through the cold winter night. Nor was he willing to give up his charge once it had been delivered safely into human hands. As Ida carried the child across the field back to the house, the cat followed at her heels.

At first, Ida's mother refused to allow the animal into the house. But after her children recounted the story of protective behavior, she relented. "Or rather," Ida is quick to clarify, "she didn't so much give in as stop refusing to let us let him in. She didn't think much of the idea of a cat in the house, but she recognized a good deed when she saw one." The cat seemed to grasp the rules immediately. Rather than jump up on the table, where Ida's mother had laid the child for a closer examination, he simply stood at polite attention a few feet away, where he could watch the proceedings without getting in the way.

Despite the hardship of raising an extra child, Ida's parents were determined to foster the infant, at least for a while. Ida suspects her parents knew whose child he was and believed that one day—perhaps when times improved—his real parents would come forward to claim him. Ultimately, they adopted the boy, formally giving him the name Joe, as in Joseph from the Christmas story. "Because he came to us so close to Christmas," Ida explains. "We called the cat Christmas for the same reason, as a matter of fact. Though maybe we should have named him Santa Claus. But that would have been too confusing for my little brothers and sisters, I think."

According to Ida, Joe grew up strong and healthy—a hard worker, always willing to pitch in. "I'm sure he was grateful to my parents for taking him in," she adds, "even though it's still not the happiest of endings. We lost him in Korea, when he was just shy of twenty years old."

And what of Christmas?

"He was a barn cat," Ida replies. "He never liked being in the house much. It probably cramped his style.

Once he knew Joe was all right, he preferred going back to the barn. He made a nice place for himself there and kept the mice away during the summer. And of course, every Christmas he got a bowl of milk or a helping of turkey—a special little present all his own."

The Plague Years

THOUGH CATS MAY HAVE BEEN held in high regard during the early centuries of human civilization, they fared rather less well after the fall of the Roman Empire. As political and religious dictators jockeyed for power, ordinary citizens soon learned that independence and ingenuity became rather dangerous characteristics to display. Unfortunately, cats have never been able to hide their intelligence; and as a result, they earned the distrust of most people. For the next several hundred years, cats were routinely rounded up and burned, skinned, boiled, or drowned.

In so doing, the citizens of Europe unwittingly fostered a resurgence in the rodent population—the consequences of which proved to be devastating. Rats entering European harbors from the Orient were infected with bacteria now known to cause bubonic plague. The disease was actually transmitted by fleas that had ingested the blood of infected rodents. Within a week of being bitten by an infected flea, the human victim developed a high fever, began vomiting profusely, and quickly fell into delirium. Lymph nodes, particularly in the groin and the thighs, swelled painfully. In most cases, death occurred within a few days.

The first outbreak, in the fourteenth century, destroyed nearly half the population of Europe, or about 75 million people. Several subsequent epidemics proved no less destructive. Almost two centuries passed before the general population realized that the most effective way to stop the plague was to control the rodent population. In desperation, the citizens of Europe turned to the feline species for assistance—and though much maligned, the humble cat willingly agreed to help. While never quite rehabilitated to the divine status they enjoyed in Egypt, cats were once again allowed to flourish; and as they grew fruitful and multiplied, the rat population dwindled proportionately. For better or worse, humanity was once saved by the humble house cat.

5

MY BEST
FRIEND IS A CAT

THE IDEA THAT CATS AND DOGS naturally despise one another is profoundly inaccurate. Problems of language underlie many of the disagreements observed between cats and dogs. Perhaps the reader has either observed or experienced firsthand the frustration associated with responding to questions posed by someone who speaks a different tongue. Though many attempts resolve themselves peaceably, with a good deal of smiling and head-bobbing all around, a surprising number escalate into shouting matches, complete with finger-pointing or other animated gestures.

Cats and dogs share a number of common signals, but the meaning accorded each sign often differs widely. Cats, for example, usually wag their tails to express confusion or frustration, while dogs use the same signal to express joy or a desire to play. Whereas cats tend to interpret quick movements as signs of aggression, dogs are more inclined to leap or jump as a form of play. Anyone, moreover, who has spent time around cats has probably observed the effect a loud noise—such as the piercing bark of a Pomeranian—can have on the feline nervous system.

Cats and dogs reared in the same household tend to pick up each other's language rather quickly, and youthful ingenuity usually repairs the occasional breach of communication. Young members of either species, often learn to read the most common signals thrown out by an older dog or cat. By the same token, if given proper respect, an older animal will rarely resort to force to prove a point.

A number of conflicts between cats and dogs arise from personal or territorial boundary misunderstandings. From the feline perspective, dogs have no sense of personal space whatsoever: They persist in snuffling and snorting around one's unmentionables and clamoring for physical closeness. From a dog's point of view, cats are the Attila the Helpless of the four-legged set, pretending that they *didn't mean* to steal your food while you were distracted by the postman, or to slice your nose because you happened to say hello a little too loudly first thing in the morning.

Certain breeds are more likely to fight than others. Greyhounds, for example, are trained to run down anything that even remotely resembles a rabbit; and God help the poor

soul who comes between a bulldog and his dish. Devon Rex cats, meanwhile, frankly prefer associating with people rather than other animals—perhaps because their fragile coats and slight build make fraternizing with lively dogs a bit of a dicey proposition. Still, with time and supervision, many breeds can learn to live together peaceably. In certain cases, cats and dogs can even develop relationships characterized by a profound and touching affection.

Rough Rider

According to Heidi Kuntz, of Wheeling, West Virginia, Pod has loved the outdoors since he was a kitten. Of course, he's perfectly happy to come inside to eat, sleep, or lounge by the fireplace. Occasionally, he'll even condescend to pass judgment on the television fare offered up on the hundred-odd channels supplied by the Kuntz's satellite dish. As often as not, he'll demonstrate his disgust with the currently airing program by sitting atop the television set and allowing his tail to droop disdainfully in front of the screen. Like many felines, he appears most offended by commercials involving cats—perhaps because they're regularly depicted in a demeaning light as finicky, sneaky gluttons.

Pod seems to feel that the world beyond the four walls of the Kuntz home offers far more interesting entertainment. The house is situated on fifty acres, after all, and is populated by a wide range of fascinating creatures, including birds, squirrels, possums, raccoons, and insects of both the winged and multilegged varieties. There's also a stable inhabited by two horses, a colt, and a billy goat. Fifty acres represents a handsome kingdom for a cat of any size, but making the rounds and tending the perimeter does make for a rather enormous responsibility, what with all the trees to climb, bushes to mark, and secret places to explore.

Aegis entered the Kuntz home when Pod was a little more than a year old. An extremely amicable puppy of rather undistinguished bloodlines, Aegis quickly settled into the daily rhythms of the Kuntz family life. Pod seemed to feel that Aegis's social training required a few swats on the nose, after which the puppy seemed to grasp certain matters of protocol a bit more clearly: For example, the backside of a cat may be investigated only upon invitation, never at random, and no canine may ever approach a feline who is engaged in performing his toilet. Once these and a few similar rules of conduct had been firmly memorized, relations between Pod and Aegis settled into a respectful formality.

Judging by his cool behavior toward the new puppy, neither Heidi Kuntz nor her husband Jeff would have suspected Pod of harboring anything but a detached amusement for Aegis. Perhaps he felt some sympathy over the fact that, when out of doors, the dog was compelled to spend unsupervised afternoons

on a chain. Perhaps he simply believed that whoever lived within the confines of *his* territory and regularly enjoyed the affection of *his* human companions entered into the sphere of *his* responsibility. Perhaps Pod's demeanor simply exemplified the old cliché about still waters running deep.

In any case, one summer afternoon while Aegis was still a puppy, Heidi was interrupted from her household chores by the sound of animated barking in the front yard. Peering out the front window, she was horrified to see a large, snarling German shepherd slowly approach Aegis—who had stretched his chain to the limit in his instinctive attempt to defend his territory from the interloper. Heidi reached for a broom and had just thrown open the front door to shoo the intruder away when she was arrested by an incredible sight.

"Just as the dog was about to jump on Aegis, something that looked like a rock seemed to fall right out of the sky on top of him," she explained. "But then whatever it was seemed to wrap itself around the dog's neck and the dog started howling, and all of a sudden I realized it couldn't be a rock—it was Pod. I looked up, and I could still see the leaves shaking on the branch of the tree he'd jumped down from. I guess he waited until that dog was right underneath him, and then he just fell on top of him and with his claws out and teeth exposed. I don't know if the dog started howling out of pain or because Pod just scared the you-know-what out of him."

Almost instantaneously, Heidi realized that Pod—no matter how brave or indignant that anyone had dared to challenge his authority—was no match for the big dog. Before the situation deteriorated any further, she ran down the front steps of the porch and used the broom to shoo the dog out of the yard. Pod dropped off the intruder's back but stood his ground at the base of the tree from which he'd leapt.

"His fur was standing on end," Heidi recalled. "It was the funniest sight—his tail alone was about as big around as my arm. If my heart hadn't been pounding so fast, I would have laughed."

She took both Aegis and Pod into the house, and after satisfying herself that neither animal was hurt, called the local animal control society to let them know that a strange dog was wandering the neighborhood. Since that day relations between Aegis and Pod have become visibly warmer. Though Aegis is still shy of approaching when Pod is cleaning himself, the two have been observed curled around each other at nap time and occasionally tossing a ball back and forth across the floor to while away a rainy afternoon.

"To tell you the truth," Heidi reflected, "I don't think Pod's attitude toward Aegis really changed all that much after the attack. He probably always felt in some way protective, kind of like an older brother, even though he pretended to be so cool. I just think that day he blew his cover." She laughed. "And after that, there was no turning back. He couldn't pretend it never happened."

Respect

SOME ACTS OF HEROISM are subtler than others. At first glance, the story of Frankie and Johnny may not impart the same thrill as more flamboyant acts of courage. Yet in an age when respect for one's elders frequently gives way to exasperation, one cat's attempt to help his canine friend can teach us a great deal about the meaning of selfless service.

Frankie, a predominantly Labrador mix, was already getting on in years when Johnny became a member of the Watson household. Adopted from a Massachusetts shelter, the gray and white tabby kitten seemed instinctively to know his place in the social scheme and never rose to challenge Frankie's authority. According to their human companion, Geoff Watson, Frankie appeared at once amused and protective of the new member of the family.

"For a while, Johnnie seemed to bring out the puppy in Frankie," Watson recalled. "Watching the two of them play was pretty hysterical. Frankie would wait around one side of the kitchen door, inching his front paw back and forth, and Johnny would be on the other side, hunched over and wiggling his rump before *pouncing*. Then they'd gallop around the apartment chasing each other. And when Johnny got tired, he'd fall asleep between Frankie's front paws. Frankie would just lie there—sometimes staring up at you with these big, sad, doggy eyes, as if to say he'd give anything to be able to get up and go to the bathroom, but he just couldn't bring himself to wake up the baby."

Even after Johnny left kittenhood behind and grew into a fine, handsome cat, he retained an affectionate relationship with Frankie. As often as not, he'd leap on the back of the couch to look out the window when Geoff took Frankie outside for a walk, and he'd still be sitting there when they returned. The two still took long naps with each other—though Johnny eventually opted to lay against Frankie's flank or back rather than between his paws. They even ate their meals side by side, without interfering with each other's habits or investigating one another's fare.

In time, the inevitable occurred: Frankie grew old. His eyesight started to fail and he developed a cataract in one eye. By the age of thirteen, his back legs had grown so weak

that he could barely stand, and Geoff would often come home and find the poor dog lying haplessly in a puddle of urine. Eventually, Frankie was fitted with a diaper.

Oddly enough, though he seemed to be eating less, Frankie wasn't losing any weight. Geoff thought he'd hit on the reason when, upon coming home from work, he'd find Johnny's dry cat-food bowl sitting empty beside the big pillow that served as Frankie's bed. Evidently, the dog was stealing food from his feline friend. Geoff reprimanded him several times, but the food kept disappearing. It wasn't until he moved Johnny's bowl to the kitchen counter that he learned the truth.

"For the next few days, I'd come home and find the bowl on the floor," Geoff explained. "The food would be scattered everywhere, and while I was sweeping up, I realized some of it seemed to lead in a kind of trail right toward Frankie's bed. I started to worry that the whole food-stealing problem might be more serious than I thought. It's practically impossible to correct a dog when you're not around to catch him in the act—and on top of that, Johnny would probably start getting upset enough to start acting up in his own way. So not only would I have an aging dog to deal with, but a pissed-off, starving cat."

Finally, on the weekend, Geoff thought he'd watch and wait. With any luck, he'd catch Frankie knocking the food off the counter, and be able to reprimand him at a point when the dog would be most likely to learn. Instead, he fell asleep on the living room couch, and didn't even hear the bowl clatter to the floor.

"I probably registered it unconsciously," Geoff recalled. "It couldn't have been too long afterward that I woke up to hear this strange sort of *skittering* sound. I couldn't imagine what it was."

Craning his neck to peer into the kitchen, Geoff immediately noted the overturned bowl. What he wasn't prepared for, however, was the sight of Johnny standing by the bowl, literally batting kernels of dry cat food across the kitchen floor toward Frankie's bed. Whenever a kernel rolled close enough to the bed, Frankie leaned over and gobbled it up.

"All this time I thought Frankie was stealing food," Geoff concluded, "and it was actually Johnny feeding him. I could have wept. I *should* have wept. But Johnny looked so serious, I had to laugh."

Two months later, after his veterinarian discovered a tumor in the dog's chest, Frankie was gently put to sleep. For a long time afterward, Johnny padded through the apartment, crying for his old friend—often standing on Frankie's bed and kneading the pillow for a quarter of an hour at a time. At first, Geoff was reluctant to act on a friend's suggestion that he adopt a new companion for Johnny. After several months, however, Geoff brought a scruffy, black and white puppy named Appleseed home from the same shelter where he'd acquired Johnny.

"It's just like old times," Geoff said. "The dog waits on one side of the kitchen door and the cat waits on the other. One of them pounces, then they're off to the races. Then after a while, they curl up together and fall asleep. It's nice to see that continuity. All I can say is, one of them had better be around to push food across the floor for *me* when I'm old and half blind and wearing nothing but a diaper!"

Tramp and Lady

BEFORE THE READER formulates an egregiously incorrect impression, it should be made clear that the name Tramp—in this instance, at least—does not in any way reflect the moral character of the cat who bears it. The name actually refers to the appearance of the feline in question, when he arrived one late autumn afternoon at the home of Matt and Surya Drummond of Barclay, Pennsylvania.

"He was filthy," Matt Drummond recalled. "His hair was matted, he was covered with burrs and twigs. I couldn't even tell what color he was till we got him cleaned up. It looked like he'd been living in the woods for a long time."

Indeed, the Drummonds live in a pleasant, rural area, where broad fields are occasionally broken by thick patches of evergreen, elm, and hemlock. Not far from their house runs a wide stream that eventually feeds into the Delaware River. Frequent trips down to the stream became a regular part of the Drummonds' daily life when Lady, a golden retriever, joined the Drummond household about a year after Tramp arrived. "It was only fair," Matt explained. "I'm more of what you'd call a cat person, and we had Tramp, and Surya's more of a dog person, so we got Lady."

For the most part, Tramp and Lady shared a peaceful coexistence. Both animals went their separate ways, with occasional spats breaking out over the claim to a particularly engaging patch of sunlight or the rightful ownership of a rubber ball. Despite the warmth and familiarity of a pleasant home, Tramp never lost his attraction to the natural world and would complain bitterly if forced to stay inside all day. Still, Surya made sure that he came inside at night. The surrounding woods were full of foxes and other small wild animals, and she worried that Tramp might be hurt in a fight or caught in one of the metal traps laid by local hunters.

Accordingly, when Lady—barely more than a puppy—slipped out of her collar, Surya feared the worst. Although she could make out canine footprints in the mud along the banks of the stream near their home, she couldn't tell if they were Lady's or where they led. When Matt came back from running errands in town, he joined his wife in exploring the woods and fields around the stream. Though they continually called Lady's name, and asked passersby if they'd seen her, the search ultimately proved fruitless. They returned home near dusk, hoping perhaps that Lady had wandered back to the house on her own. Only after night had fallen did they realize that Tramp was gone as well.

"After dinner, we sat on the back porch with dishes of dog food and cat food laid out," Matt recounted, "hoping maybe they'd be attracted by the smell. Then this thing sort of wandered up out of the field at the edge of property. All we could see was a pair of glowing eyes that wouldn't come any closer. We both called, but whatever it was just wouldn't respond. We thought maybe it was a fox or even a raccoon or something. But it wouldn't go away either. It just sort of stayed there."

Finally, Matt stepped down off the porch to investigate. To his great surprise and relief, the creature on the edge of the field turned out to be Tramp—as matted and dirty as the day he'd first arrived on the Drummonds' doorstep. However, no matter how many different ways Matt tried to call him, the cat refused to come any closer than the edge of the field. At last, Matt called Surya to bring down Tramp's dish, in hopes that the reputed feline weakness for anything that resembles food would somehow distract him from his secret purpose. As Surya approached, the cat turned and headed back into the field.

Several years after the fact, it's difficult for either Matt or Surya to recall whether instinct, intuition, or simple common sense urged them both at the same moment to creep silently after the cat rather than sprint after him. After passing through the field into a more densely wooded area, both Drummonds became aware of a distinctly canine whimper in the darkness ahead. Surya called out Lady's name and was answered by her pained but unmistakably familiar bark. Breaking into a run, they arrived in short order at the spot where Lady lay with her front leg caught in a fox trap.

Surya knelt by Lady's side while Matt worked the trap's metal jaws open. A few seconds later, she felt Tramp's rough, warm fur against her arm, as the cat pushed his way closer to make sure the rescue was accomplished as smoothly and quickly as possible. Even after Matt carried Lady out of the woods, Tramp was unwilling to abandon his charge, but insisted on jumping into the car and accompanying Lady to

the animal clinic in town. He stopped short of following the Drummonds into the animal clinic, however, waiting patiently in the car for their return. He yowled a bit when they returned without Lady, but eventually seemed to understand that if the Drummonds weren't too upset, then there was probably no real cause for alarm.

In fact, Lady came home the following afternoon, after an overnight stay at the clinic. The trap had broken her front leg, and there was some concern that the cuts she received from its teeth might have become infected. Nevertheless, after a round of antibiotics and several weeks in a cast, she was in the pink once more. Though relations between Tramp and Lady seem to have resumed their customary formality, neither Matt nor Surya are likely to forget Tramp's compassion that night.

"Throughout the whole ride to the clinic," Surya later recalled, "he stayed in the backseat right next to Lady. Whenever we stopped for a red light, she'd lean over and touch Lady's nose with her own, or try to lick the blood off her front paw. I've never seen a cat, before or since, behave so tenderly toward another creature. I used to think they were pretty selfish, but now—I guess you'd say I'm a believer."

Blood Brothers

Dogs aren't the only animals to benefit from random acts of feline kindness. In matters both great and small, cats are known for their willingness to come to the aid of other cats. In the wild, of course, caring for members of the same tribe usually delivers immediate and obvious survival benefits. Such a sensible approach to familial relations has continued more or less intact within the gentler domesticated setting. Although exceptions to the rule naturally occur from time to time, the incidence of long-standing resentment or familial aggression is much lower among cats than among reputedly more advanced species.

Among the more distinguished examples of familial love is the case of Puff and Stuff, two brothers who began life in very harsh circumstances indeed. Most sensible souls will agree that a city street is hardly a proper home for children. Yet Puff and Stuff were abandoned in an alley just west of New York City's 42nd Street. Little more than two weeks old, the brothers had been left to fend for themselves in a cardboard box beside an overflowing dumpster. At such a tender age, kittens are unable to eat solid food, and they depend for nourishment on their mother's milk. The tiny creatures weren't even old enough to regulate their body temperature and desperately needed the warmth of their mother's body to keep from freezing. Had a passerby not heard Puff's mournful cry of distress, the two would surely have perished within a matter of hours.

The good Samaritan immediately brought the kittens to a neighborhood pet store that routinely takes in stray or rescued animals. The owner, Janice Regan, was surprised when she opened the box to find that little orange and white Puff had wrapped himself protectively around his brother. When she reached inside the box to examine the kittens, Puff actually gave a warning hiss and began to scream frantically when separated from his brother. Stuff, by contrast, was too weak to offer much response. The best he could do was open and close his mouth, barely emitting a dry, hungry squeak.

After quickly examining the kittens for wounds and broken limbs, Regan brought them to a local veterinarian. A more thorough examination revealed that Stuff, the smaller

and weaker of the two, was suffering from a respiratory infection. Illnesses of that sort are often fatal even under the best of circumstances. Stuff's survival was due almost entirely to his brother's protection. The veterinarian was sure that Puff was also infected, and didn't expect either kitten to survive the night.

Against all odds, both Puff and Stuff responded to their medication. For the first few days of treatment, Puff remained fiercely protective of his weaker brother—allowing himself to be pried away only when it was time for a bottle feeding. By the time the kittens were returned to Regan's pet store, Stuff had grown visibly more alert; by the end of the week, both males were frolicking in the front window. Shortly after they were weaned from the bottle, the kittens were adopted into the same home by someone Regan was sure would care for them as tenderly as they deserved. Her instincts proved correct. A year later, she received a brief note of thanks from the cats, and a photograph showing two healthy toms sharing a friendly cuddle.

Flower Power

MILLIE AND MIKE weren't even a gleam in their mother's eye back in the late 1960s, when hundreds of young people across the United States sought to end war by passing out flowers. Echoes of the peace movement can still be felt today in California, where the flower power movement began and where Millie and Mike were born.

The gray and white tabbies share a pleasant house in West Hollywood with their human companions, Ed Hoppit and Richard DeBonner. Like many Californians, Hoppit and DeBonner have seen their share of disturbances in recent years, from riots to earthquakes to grotesque media frenzies. They were nevertheless surprised when the threat of violence reached their own backyard one Sunday afternoon in the summer of 1996, with the intrusion of a dog of unknown origin.

On the afternoon in question, Mike was enjoying the sun on the rustic back porch of the Hoppit/DeBonner home when the intruder slipped stealthily into the backyard. Mike failed to detect a disturbance in his scent field until the dog—rapidly advancing on the porch—had cut off his only avenue of escape. Mike backed up against the French doors, puffed himself up, and began to yowl. In response, the dog commenced barking.

The argument immediately drew Hoppit's attention, and from an upstairs window, he watched the canine intruder

close in on Mike. Hoppit ran down the stairs to intervene, but before he reached the ground floor he heard a violent crash. Fearing the worst, he was surprised upon reaching the back porch to see the dog backing away from the assault. Hoppit flung open the French doors and commanded the dog to vacate the premises. Mike, meanwhile, took the opportunity to slip inside.

Once the dog had fled and Mike was safely inside, Hoppit noticed the mess on the back porch. A clay pot, which had been artfully arranged on the windowsill over-looking the porch, now lay on its side on the porch floor; soil and begonia petals were now scattered in all directions. Stepping back from the French doors, Hoppit glanced at the window. "It was hard to miss Millie's back end protruding from the sill," he recalled later, "her tail twitching back and forth like the spastic pendulum of a grandfather clock."

Gingerly, Hoppit stepped out onto the porch. Millie sat staring a few seconds longer in the direction in which the dog had fled before turning to her human com-panion. "She glanced down at the broken pot, then back at me," Hoppit reported. "Then she twisted herself around and jumped back inside the house. The way she moved, it looked for a second like she was shrugging her shoulders— as if to say, 'Sorry for the mess, but what else could I do?' And she was right, of course. I mean, if she hadn't taken the initiative and knocked over the flower pot, things might have been a lot worse."

After musing for a moment, Hoppit added, "I'm proud of the way she handled the situation in a nonviolent

HERO CATS

way. I mean, she protected her brother by throwing down a flower." He smiled. "I think she sent a very positive message to the dog: Make love, not war. It's a typical California way of working out a conflict."

The Poet's Companion

BORN IN 1722, Christopher Smart was long considered a hack writer who wrote "much uninteresting verse of second-rate quality." As a child, he was considered delicate and a bit too precocious; his rather facile gift for poetry earned him a somewhat unfortunate reputation at school. Nevertheless, he earned several prizes at Cambridge, and despite a general tendency toward drunkenness, he was awarded a fellowship there.

At the age of twenty-three, Smart moved to London, where he married the daughter of a publisher and attempted to make a living in the field of journalism. Through what have been somewhat guardedly described as "dissolute and improvident habits," he sank into financial difficulties. Shortly after his wife left him, he began suffering fits of religious mania—for which he was eventually committed for eight years to one of London's notorious, rat-infested madhouses.

The poetry Smart managed to write while incarcerated is of a decidedly extravagant quality. His visionary excess may well have been inspired by long periods of solitary confinement, during which his sole companion seems to have been a cat named Jeoffry. In return for the kindness shown him during those eight frightful years in a dank madhouse cell, Smart penned the following section of a rather long and rambling poem called "Jubilate Agno (Rejoice in the Lamb)."

> *For I will consider my Cat Jeoffry.*
> *For he is the servant of the Living God duly and*
> *daily serving him.*
> *For at the first glance of the glory of God in the*
> *East he worships in his way.*
> *For this is done by wreathing his body seven times*
> *round with elegant quickness.*
> *For then he leaps up to catch the musk, which is*
> *the blessing of God upon his prayer.*
> *For he rolls upon prank to work it in.*
> *For having done duty and received blessing he*
> *begins to consider himself.*
> *For this he performs in ten degrees.*

Christopher Smart died in 1771, eight years after his release from the madhouse. Forty years after his death, his masterwork about the famed king of Israel, "A Song to David," became the focus of intense critical attention. Although he never lived to know it, the poem earned Smart a lasting place in the ranks of esteemed British poets.

6

THE "CAT" IN THE CATASTROPHE

A
S PREVIOUSLY DISCUSSED in the preceding chapter, the tendency to claim a household—or even part of one—can sometimes give rise to disagreements between newcomers and established residents. Nevertheless, the same territorial habit can also offer some very tangible benefits. Cats, like other creatures, tend to develop a fiercely protective attitude toward their established kingdoms. They also evolve a marvelously precise map of their domain. Such maps aren't simple drawings, of course, but multidimensional sensory models, rich in details about customary smells, sounds, and temperature fluctuations. Even information concerning frequent visitors and regular occurrences eventually finds its way into a cat's sensory map of its home.

Perhaps because they live so directly within the realm of their senses, cats tend to recognize departures from the norm far more readily—and on a far more subtle level—than humans. They are quick to notice, for example, the unfamiliar scent of a strange animal. They can tell when someone has spent time in a smoke-filled room or had a bit too much to drink. They can probably discern even a few irregularities of personal hygiene. More often than not, they'll refrain from making any embarrassing accusations. Still, they usually find a way to let their companions know that potentially damaging details have been duly noted.

Defense is the chief function of this richly sensual approach to life. There are no doormen in the wild—no concierges, no buzzers, no alarms. Survival depends on a more or less complete awareness of one's surroundings at all times. One must also maintain a fairly constant alertness. Casual observers have unjustly accused felines of wasting two-thirds of every day in sleep. Anyone who has spent time in the company of a cat, however, knows that the slightest strange sound—the creak of a stair, a sigh, a gust of wind—can rouse Madame Puff from deep sleep to a state of complete attention faster than you can say Miranda.

So, though some safety experts advise homeowners to invest in elaborate electronic security systems, in many cases the most effective method to protect one's home is to invite in one of Mother Nature's most sensitive and sophisticated alarms: the humble house cat.

When a Fishy Smell Isn't Fish

SOME CALL IT KISMET; others, fate. The less mysteriously inclined might simply want to chalk it up to coincidence. To some, the events that unfolded in a Midwestern college town represent a classic tale of poisoning—a true-life, cat-and-mouse detective story, distinguished by the fact that the hero who solved the mystery and saved the lives of Ray and Carol Steiner was a real cat.

The tale begins in 1993, when Carol Steiner, a music teacher from Bowling Green, Ohio, discovered a litter of kittens outside her mother's nursing home. Because she and her husband, Ray, already shared their home with three cats, they were initially reluctant to adopt any of the foundlings. Nonetheless, one of the kittens succeeded in softening a spot in their hearts and eventually became the fourth feline member of the Steiner household. The newcomer was named Ringo, after former Beatles drummer, Ringo Starr. According to Carol, the tabby earned his moniker early on by demonstrating rather creative percussive skills. Whereas most felines tend to call attention to their needs through chirping, trilling, or other verbal antics, Ringo likes to tap his paws on the kitchen door.

The "Cat" in the Catastrophe   *111*

Several years later, Carol Steiner marvels at the good fortune of their decision to adopt the red tabby Manx. "Had we stuck to our convictions," she recalls, "we would be dead today."

Two years after bringing Ringo home, both Ray and Carol began to feel strangely out of sorts. They suffered severe headaches, bouts of nausea, and high blood pressure. Like most sensible people, the Steiners sought reasonable explanations for their disquieting symptoms. Ray, a math professor at Bowling Green University, was recovering from heart surgery, after all; and Carol had a history of allergies. Disturbingly, their conditions continued to deteriorate, with complications ranging from memory loss to difficulty staying awake longer than five or six hours a day. The idea of being slowly poisoned never entered their minds.

Desperate times often require desperate measures. Late one August afternoon, Ringo roused the Steiners from what may have been their final sleep by repeatedly slamming his body against the front door. At last, he succeeded in waking Carol, who let him outside. She watched as the tabby made his way around the south side of the house and then returned, meowing, waiting for her to accompany him. Carol's decision to follow proved the turning point in a story that may otherwise have ended in tragedy.

Ringo led Carol around the house to a landscaped area adjacent to a gas meter. Resisting his natural inclinations, the cat began digging through jagged landscaping material made up of bits of lava rock. Almost at once, the pungent odor of natural gas rose from the ground. Carol immediately telephoned the appropriate authorities, who, upon investigation, discovered an underground gas leak. Suddenly, the source of the Steiners' mysterious symptoms became clear: Methane gas fumes had been seeping through the ground into the house for months, slowly and surreptitiously poisoning the air inside their home.

Once the leak was repaired and the house was thoroughly aired, Carol and Ray's health improved dramatically. Word of Ringo's extraordinary detective work soon reached the Wood County Humane Society in Bowling Green. Without hesitation, the society nominated Ringo for the prestigious William O. Stillman Award for Bravery, bestowed by the American Humane Society. The national award is given to animals that have risked their lives to save the lives of others, as well as to humans who have rescued animals at the risk of great personal injury.

Many animals rescue their human companions in an effort to save their own lives. By leading Carol to a leak she couldn't smell and the gas meter failed to register, however, Ringo was able to alert his companions *before* disaster struck. And in so doing, Carol feels that her clever sleuth of a tabby has forever "shattered the myth that cats are indifferent."

In the Nicky of Time

A SIMILAR—AND POTENTIALLY more explosive—scenario unfolded recently in the little town of Oak Bluffs on the island of Martha's Vineyard. A favorite vacation spot of presidents and potentates, the picturesque islet off the coast of Massachusetts is also home to a native population of sailors, innkeepers, artisans—and quite a few salty cats. Nicky, one of the more quick-witted of the feline residents, shares his home with metal sculptor Barry Silberman.

Silberman discovered the black and white shorthair in an alley one frigid November morning. The unhappy feline was severely undernourished and suffering from an abscessed wound on his back leg. Barry darted into a nearby store and bought a small can of cat food. Returning to the alley, he popped the lid and gained the cat's trust and gratitude by offering him his first square meal in weeks. As the first few flakes of a spectacular snowstorm began to fall, Silberman took the shivering cat to a local veterinarian. The doctor cleaned the wound on his leg, prescribed a round of antibiotics, and pronounced the cat extremely lucky indeed. Peering out at the steadily falling snow, he said he doubted the cat would have survived the storm.

"Looks like you found him in the nick of time," he concluded.

There are, one assumes, far more specious grounds for naming a companion. Based on the doctor's comment, Silberman decided to call his new friend Nicky. Though hindsight provides a handsome symmetry to the story, no one could have predicted that Nicky would fulfill the prophecy of his name by repaying Barry's kindness in a similarly timely fashion.

For several months, Barry and Nicky happily shared a small house on the edge of town. After putting in several hours welding in his studio, Silberman returned home late one night and fell immediately into an exhausted sleep. It seemed he'd barely settled when Nicky woke him by pawing at his eyelids.

"At first," Silberman recalled, "I thought he was hungry. If I sleep past his normal breakfast time, he sometimes tries to open my eyes for me. But that morning, when I finally came to enough to focus, it was still dark in my room. So I just pushed him away and turned my face to the pillow."

Undaunted, the cat resorted to more persuasive tactics. "He pushed his nose in my ear," Silberman recalled, "and started pawing the back of my neck—acting, as my grandmother would say, like a real *nudje*."

Finally, Barry became aware of the odor of natural gas seeping into his room. Since the bedroom was located at the opposite end of the house from the kitchen—which was equipped with a gas stove—he immediately grasped that the fumes must already have filled the rest of the tiny house.

Silberman bundled Nicky in his arms and climbed out the bedroom window; he then ran across the street and knocked on a neighbor's door. Somewhat bemused to see a man clutching a cat on her doorstep, the elderly woman readily agreed to let Barry use her phone to call the fire department. Silberman credits Nicky with helping to convince his neighbor of the seriousness of the situation.

"If I wasn't holding Nick," he explained, "I'm not sure she would have let me inside at four o'clock in the morning. I guess someone with a malicious intent would probably not carry a cat with them."

Firefighters quickly arrived on the scene and discovered that the pilot light in Silberman's stove had blown out. So much gas had accumulated inside the tiny cottage that the slightest spark could easily have touched off an explosion. After opening the windows and doors to thoroughly air the house, the pilot light was reignited without incident.

"You were lucky," one of the firefighters told Barry after he and Nicky returned home. "You got out just in the nick of time."

Nicky, enjoying a bowl of milk at that moment, quite sensibly resisted comment.

Hail, the
Mighty Firefighters

A NUMBER OF DOMESTIC CATS have proven themselves extremely vigilant in detecting fires. One of
the earliest feline recipients of the coveted William O. Stillman
Award, for example, was a Burmese cat named Samantha, who
saved her companions from an apartment fire. As a result of her
timely alarm, her companions were able to call the fire department and alert other building residents to the danger. More than
forty lives were spared that night.

Some felines are not quite as lucky as others. Though
they managed to save the lives of their companions, they themselves perished in the blaze. Among the fallen, we may count the
following brave hearts:

Morris, a St. Paul, Minnesota, resident, whose howls alerted his
companion to a fire that broke out in the tavern below their
apartment in 1986. Morris's cries enabled his companion, Irene
Machenhausen, and her next-door neighbor to escape with their
lives. The Associate Press report noted, however, that Morris
himself was trapped by flames in a second-story hallway.

Puff, whose Fredonia, Wisconsin, home was destroyed by flames
driven by fifty-mile-per-hour winds. According to a 1987 *Chicago
Tribune* report, Puff alerted his companion, Carol Briemon, by
scratching on her bedroom door. She awoke in time to urge five

other residents to escape just before the roof of the house collapsed. Tragically, Puff's charred body was later found among the ruins.

Kitty, a stray adopted by seventy-four-year-old Eva Chesney only months before fire spread through her Stevens Point, Wisconsin, home in the winter of 1986. Alarmed by clouds of thick smoke rising from the basement, Kitty woke her companion by scratching on the bedroom door. As reported by the Associated Press, Chesney didn't realize that Kitty hadn't followed her outside until after she'd telephoned the local fire department. Firefighters found Kitty on the ground floor, where she'd succumbed to smoke inhalation.

Another brave **Morris,** whose cries woke Grantham, North Carolina, homeowners Jim and Jennifer Cox in time to whisk their two daughters to safety. Mrs. Cox told Associated Press reporters that although they called to the cat as they made their escape, he didn't follow. His body was later recovered by firefighters.

Not all tales of feline vigilance end tragically, of course. Thomas Taylor of Oakland, California, reports that his cat—a gray tabby named Mouse—sat on his chest one night in November 1996 and meowed repeatedly until he woke up. With a week to go before Thanksgiving, Taylor had been in a hurry to finish renovations to the family kitchen before the holiday season commenced in earnest. A stray electrical spark came close to stifling any thoughts of celebration, however, by igniting a bag full of varnish-soaked rags next to the refrigerator.

Thick smoke had already filled the kitchen and was making its way through other downstairs rooms when Taylor grudgingly rose from his warm bed to investigate the reason for Mouse's distress. The timely alarm gave Taylor an opportunity to rouse his wife and two children and escape the house before the fire spread. "It wasn't till we were inside our next-door neighbor's house that I realized I was clutching Mouse to my chest. I don't even know how or when I picked him up. My neighbor just sort of looked at me funny and said the cat might be able to breathe better if I wasn't holding him so tightly. I guess in my panic I was squeezing him pretty hard."

Thanks to Mouse's early warning, damage to the Taylor home was confined to the kitchen and two adjacent rooms on the lower level. Even though repairs meant more extensive renovations than Taylor had originally intended, he and his family rang in the holidays with greater cheer than they'd ever felt before. Food, supplies, and other assistance donated by friends and neighbors gave the end of the year celebrations extra poignance.

"The meaning of Thanksgiving was really driven home to us that year," Taylor explained. "We had so much to be grateful for—our lives, our home, our friends, and especially our cat. I can't imagine what would have happened if Mouse hadn't taken it upon himself to wake me up."

Of course, Mouse was rewarded handsomely for his conscientiousness. He had his own platter of holiday turkey, and his Christmas stocking was filled to the brim with toys sent by well-wishers from around the entire neighborhood. According to reports, he's already preparing his list for next year.

Once Is Not Enough

MOST PEOPLE WOULD consider themselves lucky to have been spared merely once in their lives by a timely feline warning. Yet in the space of little more than two weeks, fortune—in the form of a gray and white cat named Crosby—smiled twice on Maria Barney. Needless to say, the former Pittsburgh resident feels an enormous debt of gratitude toward her watchful companion.

Maria adopted Crosby in 1975, and for several years the two shared the top floor of a three-story home in Pittsburgh, where Maria pursued a career in acting. Since her housemates worked during the day, Maria frequently took advantage of the silence around the house to catch up on her sleep. One afternoon, she was awakened by the noise of Crosby skittering around and around the bed. The agitated feline even went so far as to leap several times on the bed in an effort to gain Maria's attention. Finally, Crosby sat on the edge of the bed, staring at her somewhat attentive companion until she was absolutely certain eye contact had been established. Then, very slowly she turned her gaze to the window at the foot of the bed.

Maria followed her stare and was alarmed to see a reddish glow lighting up the glass. Rising cautiously, she made her way to the window and lifted the curtains. A raging fire had broken out in the parking lot below, and was traveling quickly from car to car. From her vantage point three stories above, Maria could see that the only car that had not yet caught fire was her own. She quickly telephoned the fire department, and then raced downstairs to move her vehicle.

Years later, she can still feel the terror of the experience. "Cars were crackling and hissing all around me," she recalls. "I was sure any second one of them would explode. Later, one of the firefighters told me that cars only explode like that in the movies. Still, if Crosby hadn't awakened me when she did, my car would have been destroyed along with the others."

Barely a month later, Maria was again awakened from an afternoon nap by Crosby leaping up and down across the bed. This time, the cat's distress seemed clearly inspired by the thunderstorm raging outside. Despite Maria's efforts to calm her, Crosby refused to settle down. Using the same tactics that had proven successful a month earlier, she drew her companion's attention to one of the windows at the front of the apartment. To her surprise, Maria saw that a tall pine tree in front of the house had been struck by lightning. Flames from the branches had already ignited the eaves of the roof covering the front porch two stories below. Once again, Maria was able to summon help before disaster spun out of control.

"I'll never forget the look on her face," Maria recalls with amazement. "She was so intent on locking eyes with me

before turning to the window, just to make sure she had my complete attention."

After two close encounters with disaster, Maria followed the only sensible course of action and left Pittsburgh. She and Crosby shared a comparatively peaceful life for the next ten years until 1994, when Crosby passed beyond the realm of catastrophe at nineteen years of age.

HERO CATS

And the Waters Swelled

LEST THE READER be tempted to believe that cats respond only to disasters involving ghastly fumes or flames, the tale of Crusher may provide an arresting counterpoint. The eleven-pound orange tabby shares his home with Mark and Joy Lussier of Salem, Massachusetts. "Crusher definitely chose us," recalls Joy Lussier of their visit to Angel Memorial Shelter in Boston. "He kept reaching his paw through the cage as if to say, 'Take me, take me.'"

And what a paw it is: Crusher is one of those rare individuals blessed with six toes on each front paw. He's also enormously personable and enjoys rewarding his companions for their attention by responding when called, fetching toys, and performing similarly amusing feats.

The power in Crusher's paws made it difficult for Joy to ignore the anxious prodding that woke her at about 2:00 A.M. one recent morning. "Crusher was sitting on my chest—which was very unusual—just kneading away and purring, trying to get my attention. When I was awake enough to focus, I thought I could hear the sound of rushing water. In itself, it's not an unpleasant sound. Unfortunately, it seemed to be coming from *inside* the house."

Joy woke her husband, who ventured downstairs to investigate. Moments later, Mark discovered that a high-pressure hose attached to the washing machine in the kitchen had broken, and water was already flooding the kitchen and basement. After shutting off the main water line, the Lussiers began bailing out the flooded areas by hand.

Precisely why Crusher took it upon himself to wake his companions remains a mystery. "He could have just waited in a dry spot upstairs till we woke up and dealt with the problem," Joy admits. "Instead, he sensed there was something not quite right about all that water gushing through the kitchen, and decided to let us know about it. We're glad he did, too —otherwise, the damage would have been much more severe."

Crusher's motive in sounding the alarm probably has a great deal to do with the pride with which most cats view their territory. Their home is their kingdom, after all, and woe betide anyone or anything that dares to rearrange the terrain without express permission of the monarch. On the other hand, it's possible that even a cat knows how hard it is to find a plumber willing to make house calls at two in the morning.

Smoke Detector

WHENEVER THE SUBJECT of guard animals arises, the names most frequently cited are overwhelmingly canine. Various hounds come to mind, along with Doberman pinschers, Rottweilers, and Great Danes. Rarely does the phrase "longhair cat" strike the listener's ear. In this context, the story of Smoke—a resident of Hartford, Connecticut—serves as a potent reminder of the protective inclinations of the feline species.

Smoke entered his companion Eliza Rivera's life more by chance than by design. Eliza's cousin had gone to great trouble to adopt the blue and white Maine Coon from a reliable breeder–only to discover that his stepdaughter was allergic to cats. Rather than return Smoke to the breeder, or offer him for adoption, he decided to make inquiries among his family members. Because Eliza's longtime feline companion had recently died, she leapt at the opportunity to adopt a new friend. Her apartment on the outskirts of Hartford seemed far too empty without the pitter-patter of feline feet.

Even as a kitten, Smoke demonstrated marked protective instincts. He'd growl whenever maintenance workers or delivery persons approached the door of Eliza's apartment, and he hovered defensively around his companion's feet whenever visitors paid a call. "Smoke is definitely a one-person cat," Rivera says. "He'll tolerate guests, but he won't go out of his way to make them feel welcome. He can be quite jealous, too, sometimes plopping himself down right between me and whoever's visiting at the time."

Though first-time visitors find Smoke's company manners somewhat unnerving, frequent guests have learned to accept his single-minded devotion to Eliza. She herself came to appreciate the cat's protective instincts all the more deeply after returning home one afternoon in the winter of 1995. She'd been feeling ill all morning, and left work several hours earlier than normal.

"Usually, he comes right up to me as I come through the door," Eliza explains. "He follows me around as I hang up my coat and so on, talking a blue streak, asking about my day and telling me about his."

On this particular afternoon, however, Smoke sat hunched and growling at the far end of the foyer. At first, Eliza thought he might be ill or wounded—a suspicion that grew stronger when the cat hissed at her approach. As she bent down to see what was the matter, he emitted a high-pitched, angry growl. Though nothing immediately seemed amiss, Smoke continued growling and hissing—even going so far as to lash out with his paw every time Eliza attempted to cross the foyer into the living room.

"I don't know how long it took me to realize what was wrong," she recalls. "All I remember was seeing the living room curtains blowing in the wind—which was strange, because I never leave any windows open when I'm out of the apartment. Then all at once it hit me that the window led to the fire escape. Someone had broken into the apartment, and Smoke

was acting so strangely because the burglar was *still there.*"

Eliza immediately scooped Smoke up in her arms and backed out into the hall. She made her way down to a neighbor's apartment and telephoned the police, who apprehended the intruder as he was making his way down the fire escape. Aware that he'd been discovered, the thief had merely hoped to get away with the few pieces of jewelry he'd stuffed into his pocket.

"I was very lucky," Eliza admits. "If I hadn't surprised him by coming home early, he would probably have cleaned out the apartment. But if Smoke hadn't been there to warn me—if he hadn't kept me from getting past the foyer—well, I just shudder to think what might have happened. All I can say is that he's as smart and as brave as any guard dog I've ever heard of."

After the incident, Rivera installed a gate across the living room window. When a friend suggested she post a Beware of Cat sign as well, however, Eliza declined.

"Why warn them?" she asks mischievously. "Smoke is my secret weapon. And isn't the whole point of a secret weapon to take someone by surprise?"

The Legend of the Birman

GOLDEN-HAIRED, with deep brown markings, white paws, and sapphire-blue eyes, the Birman is a singularly handsome breed. Of course, it's only to be expected that its exotic coloring should arouse a certain degree of speculation—particularly because the Birman's true history has been lost. The most persistent legend traces the origin of the breed to a temple in southeast Asia, built by the Khmer tribe in honor of a golden, blue-eyed goddess by the name of Tsun-Kyan-Kse, whose primary function was to preside over the passage of souls from one world to the next.

According to legend, Mun-Ha, the chief temple priest, often knelt in meditation before a solid gold statue of the goddess. His constant companion was a temple cat by the name of Sinh, a predominantly white fellow with dark ears, nose, tail, and legs, symbolizing the impurity of contact with the earth. One night, a mysterious band of raiders attacked the temple and killed Mun-Ha. As the priest died, Sinh leapt on top of his fallen master to protect the old man's soul as it fled his body. Instantly, the cat's white hair turned golden, and his yellow eyes changed to sapphire-blue. His paws, which acted as a conduit for the high priest's spirit, were transformed to the purest white. The next morning, the priests who had survived the raid were amazed to find that the remaining temple cats were similarly transformed.

Sinh would not leave the spot where Mun-Ha fell until he himself died seven days later. Faithful even in death, the cat carried his master's soul to the celestial realms. The legend concludes with the charming, though difficult to prove, detail that every temple cat who died thereafter was accompanied to heaven by the soul of a departed priest.

7

HEALING PAWS

OR THOUSANDS OF YEARS, humans have trod a
thin line between their impulse to nurture animals and their desire to eat them. The obvious
survival benefits of the latter instinct have gone largely unques-
tioned. By contrast, the long history of emotional attachment
to animals seems to have been the subject of some embarrassment in many circles.

Many learned individuals have pointed to the *essential
usefulness* of certain domesticated creatures. Dogs, for example, are adept at hunting, herding, pulling sleds, and a host of
other interesting activities, while cats protect against vermin
and other unpleasant interlopers. Such service, it's argued,
generates a desire to nurture and safeguard the animals who
provide it. Another hypothesis claims that certain domesticated species awaken a type of parental instinct. Dogs and
cats in particular are warm, round-eyed, and pleasant to
hold—and like human infants, they emit mildly intelligible
cries, gurgles, and other noises.

Another possible explanation may be found in the
results of a recent study by Australia's Baker Medical Research

Institute. In 1992, researchers discovered that pet owners showed lower cholesterol levels, lower levels of triglyceride fats, and lower blood pressure than people who had no pets. Research in both Australia and the United States, meanwhile, has also determined that pet owners visit their doctors less frequently than petless persons. Because health improvements are typically seen only after people adopt a pet, the evidence further suggests that the link between animal contact and human health may actually be causal.

The potential health benefits of animal companionship extend from the strictly physiological to the psychological as well. People who have adopted animals are less likely to report feelings of loneliness or depression than those without pets. Some strike up lasting friendships with other people who have pets. Children raised with animals tend to display greater emotional freedom and self-esteem than those without pets. Their animal companions often take on the role of confidante, and they rarely criticize a disorderly room, failure to study, or other childhood improprieties.

It's entirely possible, then, that the mystery of man's emotional dependence on members of the animal kingdom may hinge upon distinct physiological and psychological advantages of contact. The human body understands what the human mind cannot: Simply being around an animal can heal a broad spectrum of emotional and physical difficulties. In effect, the drive to care for animals is as closely associated with survival as depending on them for a food source.

Beyond Appearances

A N ANIMAL'S EYES have the power to speak a great language," the twentieth-century philosopher Martin Buber once observed. Few humans have enjoyed the privilege of witnessing the profound effect of this unique form of communication as closely as Sandra Campbell. A registered nurse, Campbell is a longtime volunteer with the animal-assisted therapy program sponsored by the Somerset, New Jersey, Human Society (a.k.a. St. Hubert's Giralda). Since the inception of the program in 1990, she's taken kittens from the shelter to convalescent centers, nursing homes, VA units, and senior residences in the Somerset County area, visiting patients typically considered to have passed beyond the reach of conventional medical assistance. The men and women she sees often suffer from advanced forms of Alzheimer's disease, psychiatric disorders, or irreversible physical traumas.

For several years, one of her most talented assistants has been a gray tabby named Spunky. Like the rest of the kittens who accompanied Sandra to various facilities, Spunky was returned to the shelter at the end of every visit. Unlike the others, however, the little gray fellow with ears too big for his head just couldn't seem to get himself adopted. Day after day, he watched his more attractive and outgoing compatriots carried off in the arms of excited human companions;

day after day, he was left behind, like the kid chosen last for the school baseball team.

Finally, Sandra couldn't stand the sorry spectacle any longer, and she and her husband, Barry, decided to adopt Spunky themselves. She trained the kitten to lie on a towel, which became a kind of portable "safe" zone to be taken along on visiting days. Spread out on a floor, a table, a hospital bed, or the lap of an elderly patient, the towel symbolized an appropriate place to be; Spunky sat wherever it was laid, happily accepting the attention lavished on him by grateful patients.

Staff and administrators at the facilities Spunky visited were amazed both by his serenity and by the effect he had on patients. Many of the patients he came in contact with suffered from varying degrees of agitation. Those who could still recognize their surroundings worried about their health, while those whose memories had failed suffered from the terrible anxiety and confusion that results from memory loss. With Spunky gazing up at them from their laps, patients gradually relaxed, forgot their troubles, and became focused on the present moment. Some began telling stories about cherished animal companions of their own; others felt themselves transported back to pleasant scenes of distant times.

A year or so after adopting Spunky, Sandra was working in the shelter when someone dropped off an abandoned kitten. Thunderstorms had raged all afternoon, and the tiny orange fur ball was a wet and woeful sight, positively crawling with fleas, yet purring loudly enough to be heard across the entire reception room. Later that night, Sandra happened to mention the uncomely little creature to her husband, Barry. Something in her description tugged at Barry, and he suggested that they go back to the shelter the next day "just to take a look." Anyone with even a moderate understanding of human psychology will have foreseen by this point that the Campbells did not return home empty-handed.

The little orange fur ball, impressively christened Ralph Syracuse Campbell, soon began to serve as Spunky's understudy, visiting patients when the older cat was feeling low. For several years now the pair has worked as a team, accompanying Sandra on alternate days to various residences and health care facilities. Whereas Spunky tends to

stretch comfortably out on a patient's lap, Ralph likes to play "the invisible game," tucking his face inside an elbow or a hand until he's sure his winsome, shy demeanor has completely won over whoever's holding him.

Yet despite the difference in their individual styles, both cats seem particularly proficient at drawing out patients who suffer from extreme forms of Alzheimer's or dementia. In one exemplary case, Spunky jumped onto the lap of an elderly woman who had lapsed into a completely nonverbal state. Startling the nurses who had grown accustomed to her silence, the old woman smiled down at her visitor and remarked, "Pretty cat." The following week, when Ralph stepped gingerly onto her lap, the old woman uttered her first complete sentence in years. Meeting Ralph's coyly upturned gaze, she exclaimed, "My, what a handsome cat this is!"

The mystery of silent communication between man and animal may never be fully understood. It can, however, be rewarded. In 1995, the Delta Society honored Ralph and Spunky with an award for Lifetime Achievement in the field of animal-assisted therapy. Their uncanny gift for breaking through barriers others have found impenetrable is a lesson to us all—and a sign of hope that beyond the confusing babble of grunts and cries that daily arises among the creatures of the earth, a single great language may truly unite us all.

Cat's Paw

ELLEN PETRICONE DOESN'T LIKE to talk much about her brush with death. "It was so fleeting," she explains. "And, I have to admit, it's a little painful to remember. It might not have amounted to anything, of course—but thanks to Jack, I'll never have to wonder about what might have happened."

The "Jack" in question is a white and black tom adopted as a kitten by Ellen and Alex Petricone.

"We'd been house hunting when we found him," Ellen recalls. "We were driving past a long, empty field on our way to look at our fourth or fifth house. I was just staring out the window when I saw what seemed to be a baby rat or squirrel—or even a chipmunk—climbing out of a sort of ditch between the field and the road ahead of us. I was afraid it might dart in front of the car as we drove by, so I told Alex to slow down, so we wouldn't hit the baby squirrel. Alex squinted hard, and said, 'That's no squirrel, that's a kitten.'

"So we pulled the car over and got out. I'm not sure what the poor little thing made of us, we were both trying to be as gentle and as friendly as we could—practically walking on tiptoe and talking in high, baby voices. He must have thought we were nuts. Anyway, he let out this pitiful cry when we reached him—I don't think I'd ever seen a kitten open its mouth so wide. I scooped him up, and he just about buried himself in my hair. He was shaking so hard. It was late October or early November—too cold for a little kitten to be out wandering alone."

After having Jack examined by a veterinarian, the Petricones took him home and began calling area shelters and animal agencies to learn if anyone had reported a missing kitten. They took out an ad in the local paper, and posted flyers around their small New Hampshire town. Receiving no response, they decided to adopt the kitten themselves.

Jack lived happily with Ellen and Alex in their new home for several years. Unfortunately, one rainy March evening, Alex was killed in a traffic accident while driving home from work. He was twenty-nine years old.

"It was a horrible time," Ellen remembers. "I had recently been laid off, and we'd been struggling to make mort-

gage payments, car payments, furniture payments. I just kept thinking it was so unfair. It wouldn't take a rocket scientist to figure out why—even months after Alex died—I was having trouble sleeping."

In the weeks and months following Alex's death, Jack rarely left Ellen's side. He followed her around the house, waited on the windowsill when she went out, and slept on the pillow next to her at night. Never intrusive, but plainly visible, Jack was always available when Ellen needed consolation of the furry, whiskered variety.

"Jack was really amazing," she recalls. "He'd always been an affectionate little guy, but he liked his independence, too. But after Alex died, he started showing the type of devotion you'd expect from a dog. I'd get up, he'd get up; I'd sit down, he'd sit down. He'd even follow me into the bathroom at night, and hop up on the counter beside me while I washed up and brushed my teeth."

After a particularly grueling week, Ellen found herself in extremely low spirits as she prepared for bed. "I don't know how long I'd been standing at the bathroom sink," she explains, "with this bottle of sleeping pills in one hand, and my other hand hanging open in midair. I remember thinking how defeated I felt, how I didn't think I had the strength to go on. I didn't even hear Jack jump up on the counter next to me. All I remember is that—just as it crossed my mind that I could just take the whole bottle of sleeping pills—Jack lifted his paw and sort of swatted at my open palm."

"I was so startled, I think I even jumped. I turned, and Jack was looking at me with his head cocked to one side. The look in his eyes was such a strange mix of curiosity and compassion—as though he were saying 'What are you doing? I mean, I know what you're doing, but what are you *doing?*' And all of a sudden I thought, what *am* I doing?"

"I threw away the sleeping pills and marched into the kitchen and made us both some good, old-fashioned warm milk. When I went to bed, I gave Jack a big hug, and promised that I'd never even think about leaving him again. Of course, I can't speak for Jack—but I don't think I'd slept as well in years as I did that night!"

Triumphant Trio

THE WORD THAT SPRINGS almost instantly to mind when Hector Castaner begins to talk about his three cats is *joy*. It's clear, too, that his enthusiasm is infectious. Having spent the better part of the last seven years visiting hospitals, pediatric rehabilitation centers, and nursing homes in and around Miami, Hector's cats—Buster, Flashback, and Flame—have become something of a legend in Metro Dade County. In honor of their work, they received the Delta Society's 1997 Beyond Limits Award as Therapy Animals of the Year.

"I've had the opportunity to see very sick children experience genuine joy and happiness through interaction with my cats," affirms Hector, a psychologist for Metro Dade Human Services. "Doctors and hospital staff can see this happiness recorded in every cell of their patients' bodies."

Firsthand experience contributes a good deal to Hector's unshakeable faith in the healing power of feline contact. Suffering from a particularly unstable form of diabetes for many years, Hector endured a number of physically incapacitating symptoms. A divorce, meanwhile, left him angry, depressed, and withdrawn. Finally, a friend suggested he adopt Buster from a family who was moving back to Canada and couldn't take the cat with them.

"Watching the cat walk around the house—scratching, sniffing, getting into things—woke me up," Hector explains. "I started looking at things from his point of view. I wanted to get inside his head, and so I put my face right up to his. And the funny thing is, when you really take the time to look at a cat face to face and eye to eye, it's like entering a new continent—a little scary at first, until you start doing it continuously. After a while, I found I was starting to get interested in the world again. I started to gain weight and my disease began to stabilize."

Shortly after Flashback and Flame joined the Castaner household, Hector decided to share his experience with others in need of healing. In 1994, under the guidance of the Delta Society, he developed a Feline Professional Services program, offering cat training, consultations, and pet-facilitated therapy. He began visiting shelters for abandoned children and public libraries, teaching children of all ages to love, understand, and take responsibility for animals. Though he's invested a good deal of effort in training his cats for demonstrations and shows, they don't perform stunts or tricks. Instead, they do things not ordinarily expected from felines.

"I teach them to ride comfortably in a car," he explains proudly, "and to come when they hear the keys jingling. They walk on a leash and give their paw, which amazes a lot of people—especially the kids. When I take the cats into the oncology ward, for example, the kids are so surprised. They always ask if they can take the cats for a walk down the hall. Some of them ask if they can take one of the cats with them when they go for chemotherapy—which really helps to take their mind off what's going on. When we visit the paralyzed kids in the rehabilitation center, the cats sit right on the tray table, nose to nose with the patients. The kids get to pretend they're in the jungle."

Children aren't the only beneficiaries of Buster, Flashback, and Flame's special brand of healing. Nursing home patients also get a lift from their visits. "I feel good the rest of the afternoon and night!" exclaims one wheelchair-bound resident of the Miami Gardens Care Center. "You can tell they love you because they bring their littler faces next to yours and caress you."

Hector says the response of Alzheimer's patients is particularly moving. "It's like an electric shock," he explains.

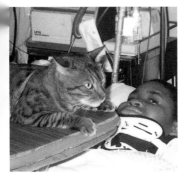

"They start talking, sharing their memories of positive experiences with cats and dogs. You can see the person inside begin to come back to the surface, and make contact with the world again."

County residents who aren't confined to health care facilities are just as likely to find themselves unexpectedly delighted by a chance encounter with Castaner and his cats. In addition to their other feats, Buster, Flashback, and Flame all enjoy the occasional day at the beach—complete with a dip in the waters and a ride on the special surfboard Hector has designed and built for them.

"Any cat can do it," Hector affirms. "All you need is time and patience. Once they know there's nothing to be afraid of, their curiosity takes over. I think that's the gift they give other people, too," he muses. "They can show you how to be curious again, and that curiosity wakes you up to all sorts of new possibilities."

Acknowledgments

A NUMBER OF HEROIC beings have sustained me throughout the creation of this book. First and foremost, I owe a huge debt of gratitude to all the wonderful people who shared their stories with me. I would also like to thank Marilyn De Toro and Marge Stein of the North Shore Animal League; Joyce Briggs of the American Humane Association; Isabel George of the People's Dispensary for Sick Animals; John Delaney of the Imperial War Museum; Gillian Murchie of the Glenturret Distillery, Ltd. A special thanks must go to Buster, Flame, and Flashback for their lively inspiration, and to all the friends and family members who contributed ideas, suggestions, and other materials from which the manuscript was woven.

Without the boundless patience and support of Lisa MacDonald, Roger Straus, and Peter C. Jones, *Hero Cats* would never have been written at all. Bob Dombroski endured with particular grace the torment of reading and commenting on every page as it emerged from the printer, while tolerating my slovenliness and degenerative social skills. Carlysle, Rocky, and Gunner found their own clever ways of maintaining my tenuous connection to the present moment—usually through demanding food, lying upon the keyboard, or commanding me to hunt for toys. I thank you all so much.